D0786723

INSIDE OUT

Also by Evelyn Lau

INSIDE OUT

reflections on a life so far

EVELYN LAU

Doubleday Canada

Doubleday Canada and colophon are trademarks.

Canadian Cataloguing in Publication Data

Lau, Evelyn, 1971–
    Inside out : reflections on a life so far

ISBN 0-385-25928-X

1. Lau, Evelyn, 1971– . 2. Authors, Canadian (English) – 20th century – Biography.* I. Title.

PS8573.A7815Z53 2001   C818'.5409   C00-932390-2
PR9199.3.L3287Z47 2001

Jacket design by Kevin Hoch/Pylon
Text design by Susan Thomas/Digital Zone
Printed and bound in Canada

Published in Canada by
Doubleday Canada, a division of
Random House of Canada Limited

Visit Random House of Canada Limited's website:
www.randomhouse.ca

FRI 10 9 8 7 6 5 4 3 2 1

CONTENTS

So we beat on, boats against the current,
borne back ceaselessly into the past.

— F. Scott Fitzgerald, *The Great Gatsby*

THE SHADOW OF
PROSTITUTION

I USED TO SAY THAT if the girl in my first book, *Runaway: Diary of a Street Kid*, showed up on my doorstep, I would not let her in. But who was she? Now, more than a decade later, I find myself still unable to read more than the occasional passage in *Runaway*, and then wincingly. It exists in the world as a document of an actual period of my life, available to any stranger with a capricious interest, and yet I am barely able to crack its covers myself. It seems as vulnerable as a fleshy, pulsing thing without a shell. I want to throw clothes over it, encase it in a suit of armour, cover it up. I want cool distance rather than the raw, stormy moment. What a different book it would have been had I waited to tell that story from the detachment of a decade later, through the clinical gaze of a professional writer rather than the urgency of a teenager. Yet even then I was something of an observer, a reporter dispatched into the explosions and turmoil of my own adolescent life. The writing was always larger than I was. I felt it to be a force for which I was merely a mouthpiece. My diary, in which I recorded every conversation, every ingested drug and flailing emotion, was the shield between myself and that life, though oddly it would later be what left me open, unprotected. I remember recording my life compulsively, forsaking sleep in order to do so, even if it was my first night's sleep in days. If I could just pin those events onto the page, all that had passed before my eyes, they would cease their clamour inside me. The evils would be harnessed and coaxed back into Pandora's box, which would be shut up tightly the moment I finally laid down my pen. They were no longer confusing events and emotions I could hardly bear to reconcile as my own, but words as neat as pins. They had happened to someone, but surely not to me. The despair, the shame, the scorching rage — later, I was surprised when people referred to the anger in the book. I could not remember feeling anger myself, but it had poured onto the page like lava.

This stranger whose life seems in so many ways foreign to mine is still inside me, her experiences knit into the fabric of all the other lived experiences before and since. But the drugs, the group homes, the constant running away — those events seem firmly consigned to adolescence, behaviours that have scarcely left a mark on the rest of my life. Recently I was in the pharmacy, and there was a man in front of me who was trying to get his prescription for Valium renewed. He was perhaps in his late twenties, with messy hair and wild eyes, and extremely agitated. In a rising voice he kept insisting to the pharmacist that he was going through a rough spell, he really needed the drugs. He said he had changed doctors, and he mentioned the name of a doctor I thought I recognized as one known among addicts for being generous with prescriptions.

Once, I must have resembled this man. I caught my reflection in the mirrored post, my expression judgmental and detached, as if what he was experiencing was nothing I had ever been through. Yet I, too, had gone from doctor to doctor, concocting ailments that might result in a scrawl on a slip of paper that could be exchanged for a handful of painkillers or tranquilizers, for hours of starry elevation or cozy blankness. But I felt no empathy for him. It occurred to me that it was harder to go from day to day in the "straight" world than it had been in his world, though the melodrama of addiction had lent each hour a kind of urgency and crisis that seemed real. I remembered staggering down tilting sidewalks high on methadone or some candy-coloured cocktail of pills, sneering at the blunt, boring faces of the ordinary people with their jobs and their houses in the suburbs and their families and what seemed their unutterably dull lives. Now those were the lives that I craved to understand, to describe in my work. Those were the lives with the shading and the subtlety, the heartbreaks and triumphs, the cruelties as well as the moments of hope.

The prostitution is what has remained, what has left its seal and shadow on everything. It has set me apart, as I had feared it would — and yet perhaps hoped it would as well, because it offered a kind of protection, a wall around me. It made relationships less possible, and while that seems something to lament, I also sometimes think it is what I deliberately designed for myself, since whenever I think of a relationship I picture being locked with someone else in a room the size of a cell. But sometimes it haunts me, and I feel a sharp punch of hurt: "Oh, do you know what *she* used to do?" people I have just met will tell me others have already said to them. And I can hear in my mind their excited, confiding voices, the looks on their faces — the part shock, part enjoyment that is titillation.

Over the years I have received numerous letters from women who have worked in the sex trade, who have gone on to marry and have children and create other lives for themselves, but who have not told their families or friends of their pasts. I never know whether to feel sad or wistful when I read these letters. Sometimes I think that is what I should have done myself. Other times it seems theirs are the saddest stories — they live in a bubble they must always fear will someday burst. They believe that the people they love most would no longer love them if they knew the truth. The love that sustains them, the whole new life they balance around themselves, is predicated on a lie. They hide their pasts because they are ashamed of what they have done.

What do you do with that feeling? Some days I am certain it doesn't exist in me, but other days I feel less than, like damaged goods, inferior. I try to forget everything valuable I learned on the streets, in order to blend in, to be new. I direct my anger at the people around me, for their hidden hypocrisies, for what they have shown me of the undersides of marriages and relationships. I want to twist them open and see the darkness spill out. There is almost a relief when it does; my world view has been confirmed, so that the shaky, unstable air suddenly stills, the buildings are upright and the windows are unbroken, and life as I know it is unchanged. I have such a hard time trusting someone who shows himself to be honourable. It is too dangerous; I would be trusting him the way the middle-aged men who buy blow jobs from teenage girls have wives who trust them, who wait for them at home with dinner in the oven, and later put on frilly lingerie in an attempt to please them.

A few years ago I had a long conversation about prostitution with a man I knew. We had gone out on a number of dates; I wasn't interested in him, but it seemed like what other women in their twenties did, and something I should do, so we went to dinners and plays and talked and I knew eventually he would go away because I had no intention of ever sleeping with him. I never know how to talk about relationships with other people — none of the women who are my friends or acquaintances have worked as prostitutes, so they talk happily about their crushes, and the men they're dating or wish they were dating, and their relationships, and sex. Every conversation ultimately ends up there. And when they turn to me, to find out what's going on in that part of my life, I feel the need to join in — even though I don't perceive sex or relationships the way they do. I still view sex as a transaction, a relationship as a trap. But I obediently chime in with my own stories of having crushes on men, or being pursued by someone, or going out on dates. It's what normal people do, I tell myself. And to explain how it is otherwise for me deflates the conversation, so that the light, bright air of girlish confidences being shared is suddenly punctured, and a silence falls.

This man I was dating was telling me about his closest friend, whom he had known for many years, and how that man would be no more likely to visit a prostitute than to flap his arms and fly. He was trying earnestly to tell me that it was not as common as I imagined, that there were men out there who behaved with honour. We were sitting in a nice restaurant, the golden wine gleaming in our glasses, and I looked at him and nodded. Not long ago that same friend of his had looked me straight in the eye and told me all about his visits to prostitutes. I listened to my date and nodded, and the wine tasted like gasoline in my throat as his whole fragile world balanced undisturbed between us.

The subject of prostitution remains always difficult, inflammatory, undebatable. People look to me for a solution or a political opinion and sometimes become angry when I fail to deliver, as if I am withholding something. I do not even wish to enter the discussion. Does one speak the language of the victim, who sees prostitution as abuse by men, or of the empowered woman who claims it to be an economic choice without any psychological ramifications? There have been enormous psychological and emotional costs for me, but I am uncomfortable with the former position, even though it could be argued that a teenager selling sex to men could be nothing but a victim.

Once, a friend of mine who has never visited a prostitute told me that he and his partner had developed a game where, during the course of their lovemaking, he would pay her to perform a sexual act. She would take the money and they would go to bed. "The first time I did that, she got so hot," he said wonderingly. "It was the hottest sex we'd had, ever." I felt more uncomfortable listening to this than if he had told me he liked having sex with farm animals. It was the encroachment of the coldness of prostitution into intimacy. But it was a fantasy for both of them, without an emotional cost; the exchange of bills must have felt illicit and edgy, and introduced a thrilling sliver of darkness to their lives. But this confession haunted me for a while, oddly. It sent a shiver through me. It was as if the window to his home had been open and the night had slipped inside.

It is the blurring of these lines, these worlds bleeding into each other, that makes me realize that the past exists inside me as ineradicably as the present. Then I see that most days I choose to pretend it isn't there. I don't want to be limited to looking at the world, at relationships, through the jaded eyes of a street hooker. I want to be flush with vulnerable emotion, to be swept with normal desire, to bruise my heart. Sometimes that does happen, but though the emotions are genuine there is, unconfessed to friends to whom I unburden myself of my infatuations, an edge of coldness, of remove. When the man I have an impossible crush on finally bends to kiss me, when he touches me, I disappear to a blank space where I am unreachable. It is a small, cold, white room where I feel nothing. This technique of detachment is so practised that it has become automatic, a built in defence mechanism, a switch that is flicked by an intimate touch. My heart breaks like an adolescent's when someone I have a crush on abandons or rejects me, and I spill my sorrow to friends, but there is something askew about this that I never really acknowledge. Perhaps I seek these situations, to try to show that I am normal. That I, too, can fall for someone wholeheartedly, and lose myself in the process. But the truth is that I never do, really. I am just glad of something to talk about, the way everyone else talks about their relationships — their desire for sex, their infatuations with impossible people, their love affairs and one-night stands. I want to join in the conversation and prove that I can participate — even though my experiences have set me apart.

For me, the past bleeds into the present. But the glass that separates the two worlds has been shattered. Somehow I live in both realms. The faces that exist in one world turn up in the other, this time well dressed and with wives by their sides. They are the same people. I used to wonder how those men were with their wives, their friends, their colleagues, their children. Now I know. Normal, mostly. Even the ones who are cruel in another context. No one guesses, no one wants to know.

No one wants to picture someone in their lives, at their dinner tables and cocktail gatherings, at the golf course or in bed beside them, in some cruel or ignominious scenario with a prostitute. Their faces contorted, the nakedness of their need. The rhythms of their panting, the noises they make. If I were to say anything, if I were to tell those stories, I would be the one ostracized. I would have violated some social code. Now I know this. It was acceptable when I was a teenager who told stories about what happened on the streets, because the lives I described existed in another world. I thought I could simply go on telling stories about my own life and the lives of others around me. But somewhere along the way a veil of polite silence fell. It was expected that my stories would now be of the imaginary kind, or about people you would never encounter other than in a furtive, dismissive way — the girls gathered on the street corners late at night, bright and shiny as birds in their latex and PVC, the faceless working-class men circling the block in their cars. Not about people you know.

One spring evening, while walking around after a dinner date with a nice man towards whom I felt no attraction, he turned to me and began telling me about his experiences with prostitutes. The time he picked up two girls and had a threesome, the low periods in his life when he would go downtown to buy sex. I kept my face blank. We walked past the glitzy, glass-fronted clothing stores, the throngs of tourists and teenagers, past street performers and beggars. Why was he telling me this? What made him imagine that I would understand, commiserate, desire him? He punched me lightly on the arm, like a pal. He looked happy. "You know, it's so great that I can tell you about things like that. Most women would freak out, they would get judgmental, and I know you wouldn't because you've been there." I giggled nervously and looked away. My heart felt like a stone. I could instantly access, like an eidetic memory, the revulsion I felt towards those men, and now this man was saying he was one of them. Any slight chance that we would ever do more than go to dinners and movies vanished. What he hadn't understood was that given my experiences I was probably more judgmental than women who had not been there. Because I could access those feelings. Because I knew what went on in those parked cars in the alley, the sour taste in my mouth and the sick feeling in my stomach, always the fear that something would go wrong, the vigilance for a suddenly changed mood, a flashing weapon, a curled fist. How I fled from myself through drugs and alcohol so I could be absent when those things were being done.

Yet prostitution was a world with which I was completely familiar. I knew how to behave no matter what situation arose, and that was more than I could say about the other world in which I constantly struggled, trying so hard to disguise the painful shyness and awkwardness I felt. It was a way to escape, tied with the alcohol and pills that helped facilitate that escape. There was a marriage between the behaviours, a ritual. It was a way of cutting off feeling, of transforming into another person, the cold person I wanted to be. Sometimes I felt so little it vaguely worried me, at the same time as it thrilled me — I felt like a field covered in snow, without a footprint or a living creature for as far as the eye could see. All the pain glittered and then dissolved. When I woke up in the morning, I began drinking, mixing Kahlua into my coffee until, by the third cup, it was mostly sweet brown liquor. I wrote and socialized during the day and at night dressed up in transparent blouses, stay-up stockings, and miniskirts. I stormed through the apartment in high heels, playing loud music that drove my downstairs neighbour to distraction, swallowing handfuls of pills and mouthfuls of whisky in the bathroom as I put on makeup. I left home a different person, through the mirrored lobby of the building, towards the taxi waiting in the circular driveway. I was the person I wanted to be: desired by men, unreachable by women, empty even to myself. The taxi sped off into the night, towards men and situations I knew, or towards strangers and places I did not. Sitting there in the back seat, legs crossed, the city passing by the window in a painted glaze, I would think, *Maybe tonight will be the night that something terrible happens*. Sometimes I thought this with a shiver of hope — something terrible to make it all stop.

Sex wasn't anything, but then it never had been for me. It was never an activity I engaged in except for money. Sometimes it was brutal and painful, rarely it startled me by being pleasant, most often it just felt repugnant, a chore to finish quickly while trying not to look like someone who couldn't wait to jump into a scalding shower or bath immediately afterwards. I squandered the money I earned in haste, eager to get rid of the memories that clung to the fleshy, humid bills. It didn't make any sense, what I was doing. If I didn't like it, if it wasn't for the money . . . but there was everything else. The compulsion of it, the way I lurched out the door of my apartment with my racing heart, the need to keep proving something over and over again. The need to keep disappearing, the hope that one of those nights I might vanish down a small hole and lose all feeling, all self, entirely.

Nothing stays the same. You grow older, you imagine another life for yourself, the fabric of the day begins to hold you more firmly than the call of the night. Your friends, who have families and normal lives, increasingly draw you into this other world, where people don't behave the way you do, and the more ties you make in this world, the more you sever in the other one. You meet someone who you long for in a way you have never longed for a man before, and sex becomes something that, unbearably, might actually mean something. The pain, the emptiness — you can handle a little more of it, incorporate it into yourself, as the months and years pass.

Something changed me, though, during that time — not only the experiences themselves but the act of writing about them. Perhaps it began even earlier, inside the family home, where there was no such thing as privacy or boundaries. Where doors were unlocked, undergarments examined, the contents of desk drawers exposed. Where I hunched tensely over my poetry in my bedroom, leaping in fear when my mother stealthily opened the door and snuck up behind me to ensure I was doing homework and not writing. Where she explored my naked body as critically as though it were her own, tugging and poking at my adolescent flesh while I detached in my mind. Later, in prostitution, it sometimes seemed that what was being done was only an echo of those moments with my mother — my body simply belonged to whoever was manhandling it at the time, while in my mind I drifted elsewhere. I grew up both at home and on the streets without a sense of where the lines should be drawn, and my writing ended up reflecting that lack. I could, without flinching, write about experiences that other people would consider too personal to reveal even to their closest friends, let alone to strangers. There seemed to be no limits to what I could reveal about myself or others in my life, no sense of where to stop.

Sometimes, walking home in the evenings, I pass the prostitutes on their corners downtown. Something flutters in my throat, a kind of panic. Their eyes are masked in makeup, their legs elongated by short skirts and stiletto heels. I remember, and I don't want to remember. I expect them to see it in my face, this memory, this mutual knowledge. I feel that the ordinary clothes in which I am dressed are a sham, an adopted disguise, along with all the other trappings of my ordinary life. That somewhere a pin could be pulled and it would all fall away, all come tumbling down. And I would land back on the street corner where, for a long time, I felt I belonged, as I had never belonged anywhere before. The jagged leap of fear upon entering a stranger's car, a stranger's home, was still less than the fear I had of being suffocated by my family, or by any other relationship. How do you explain that to someone? That the fear of dying was less than the fear of being locked up forever. That every night I went out, locking the apartment door behind me, my purse swinging from my shoulder and my heart in my throat, I was running and running and proving that no one could catch me. That no one could hurt me because I could go places and do things to myself beyond what they could do to me. That my life was my own to destroy. It was as simple as that in the end.

THE COUNTRY OF
DEPRESSION

IT BEGAN THERE, in that time between childhood and adulthood. How I loathed my life, my newly adolescent self! It was the usual resumé of teenage misery, unremarkable in the end. Everything around me seemed thick and woolly and static — the unwavering street outside the window of our little house, with a torturous glimpse of the downtown lights in the distance, like a mirage I would never reach. The pudgy flesh I was gaining from my secret food binges made me feel leaden and sluggish. The texture of my skin, the oil in my hair, my ugly, scratchy clothes — everything felt wrong, repulsive. I often prayed I would die in my sleep, so I would not have to face another day at school as an outcast. The screamed taunts in the schoolyard, the blade-sharp faces of my tormentors, popular girls with combs tucked in the back pockets of their Jordache jeans. Their hair was perm-ruffled and, in the provocative way they sashayed down the halls, it was plain they were already learning the secret language of sex. It seemed I had already lost that game, with my plastic glasses and their thick, distorting lenses, my hair that my father cut with a pair of kitchen scissors in the basement because my parents considered a professional haircut an unjustifiable expense. The clothes I wore were salvaged from my mother's trunk of clothes from China — bright polyester pants cut with flaring legs — and underneath I had on boxy, badly stitched underwear that my mother made for me from my father's old pyjamas. Undressing for gym class was a hasty, shameful ordeal. Next to the plumage of the other eleven- and twelve-year-old girls, I felt an abomination, and wanted to die.

But when I next opened my eyes there would be the familiar grey light through the window, and the depression would descend like a blanket. If it was winter it would be dark, and I would go to the kitchen to eat breakfast next to my father before he headed out on yet another of his unsuccessful job searches. The linoleum cold beneath our feet, our silent, awkward chewing. I would look at the soft slices of bread on my plate, how they broke apart under the jab of my knife with its dab of butter no matter how carefully I tried to spread it, and rage would course through my body. Why couldn't I butter a piece of bread without it falling apart? Why couldn't I be perfect? I wanted to take the entire loaf of bread in my hands, smear it with butter and honey, smash it in my hands, and hurl it against the wall. Perhaps then my father would rise from the icy lake of his torment, his unhappy eyes would focus, and he would see me.

I thought of suicide constantly; what likely stopped me was the thought of the trouble I would get into from my parents if I tried and didn't succeed. In the mean-time, every day was a small eternity to be endured. The light in my memory of this time seems always to be charcoal grey, or black. The air felt thick in my nostrils and throat, and the depression expanded to fill the days, weeks, and months with its massive, rolling fog.

I was twelve, or thirteen. Younger, even. Perhaps it went on for months, stopped for a while, then started again; perhaps it continued for years, with only days of remission in between. Why can't I remember? Time meant something different then, and what seemed like years might only have been months, or weeks. But I remember looking at a calendar on my bedroom wall on which I had crossed out the days with big ink Xs, flipping back through the months and realizing I had been depressed for most of the year. The memory of this is murky, a swamp of mornings waking in darkness, fear throbbing in a tight knot in my chest, and then the long day ahead wrapped in grey cotton. This state was different from pain, or panic, which I had known earlier — those emotions arrived, were experienced, then left like their brighter counterparts. You survived them, and they had an acuity that depression, in its muffling weight, lacked. When I was depressed I would have given anything for a sharp, precise emotion, even if it was only sadness. Depression had no edges and therefore no borders, no discernible beginning or end.

Doctors claim that serious depressions are often triggered by loss, or by an accumulation of losses. Perhaps I was mourning the loss of the time when we had been more or less happy, as families go, before my father became unemployed and retreated to the dark basement in shame, before my mother became increasingly hysterical and stalked through the house terrifying me with her unpredictable moods and preoccupations.

Before the arrival of my sister, who sat curled up in the crook of my father's arm while I watched from a sullen distance, murdering her in my mind. Perhaps I anticipated the unrecoverable loss that lay ahead, the day when as a fourteen-year-old I would walk out the door of my parents' house and never look back.

And then it went away. Or, perhaps, the depression remained but there was little room for it. I left home and tumbled into one crisis after another — drugs, prostitution, suicide attempts, sleeping on the streets. Depression was elbowed aside by the immediacy of fear, by the cartoon nausea of bad LSD trips and drug overdoses, by struggling daily to survive. In retrospect, perhaps all that behaviour was a form of self-medication. It was still better than the cotton-packed days of depression, which I learned to quickly eradicate with a handful of pills, a cupful of methadone, several tricks turned in a row.

In my early to mid-twenties the fog thinned and then seemed to lift for good. When I woke, the clear day lay ahead. I could intellectually recall the fact that I had been depressed — I restricted it to a period in my early adolescence — but could no longer feel it viscerally. It was like recalling a migraine, a pinched nerve, the time when you were at the kitchen counter and the knife slipped and sliced your finger open. You could describe it in some detail afterwards, but the memory of the pain would be less than a shadow of itself. This is how the body heals, how the mind closes over pain like scar tissue over a wound. When people I knew complained about being depressed, I had to swallow my impatience with them. I thought that at least they should have the grace to keep it to themselves, since there was nothing so dispiriting as listening to people almost lovingly explain the topology of their depression. The relentlessness of it, the iron lid over all their days. At least if they were experiencing a particular crisis there was heightened feeling, and you could offer a shoulder to cry on, a suggestion for action that they had overlooked, even a solution to their problems. Depression was something that simply went on and on, and wore out everyone around the depressed person.

I would try to sympathize by saying that I, too, had gone through a period of depression in my early teens. But that was all it was in my memory: a bleak, sluggish period, a long time ago. I never ceased to be grateful for its departure, though. I did remember that it had seemed worse than the most piercing pain, and so even when there was turmoil in my life, and grief, I was glad that it didn't devolve into depression. I began to think of that bleak band of time before running away as unique to a teenager's changing hormones and my circumstances at home; I saw myself as safely beyond its reach.

Then something happened. The doctors say that one serious depression puts you at risk for another during the course of your lifetime; two increases the likelihood of a third, and so on. You may not even be aware of the gravity of the precipitating losses at the time; you may think you are dealing with them just fine, that indeed you've dealt with a lot worse in the past. But then one morning you wake and discover that the fog has crept in overnight. It is banked out in the streets, so heavily that the outlines of the buildings in your familiar city are lost. There are no streets or mountains, no glimmer of water. It is in the room with you, pressing down over your nose and throat and almost suffocating you. You try to rise, to live your normal day, and discover that you can't get out of bed. You are as immobilized as if you had had a stroke in the middle of the night, while you slept. *But this is ridiculous*, you think. *Nothing's wrong with me. All I have to do is get up, the way I've done every other day, without thinking about it.* And yet you can't.

What happened to cause this depression? It took about a year to develop. Each loss, by itself, was not a cause for collapse. When I count them they fit on the fingers of one hand; they seem embarrassing in their slightness. Some setbacks and problems at work, several troubled relationships that ended badly. But these events occurred within a year and somehow, taken together, the impact they had was greater than the sum of their individual parts. I slid into depression, imperceptibly at first, then rapidly. I could not write for months on end, plagued instead by obsessive thoughts and memories. The depression that had been lurking — sneaking in under the closed door, around the window frames, filling my room slowly with smoke — poured in and sealed me shut inside its grey heart.

An acquaintance once described to me what it was like when her back went out and she couldn't get out of bed without considerable pain. She would lie on her mattress visualizing herself walking to the bathroom, then down the carpeted stairs to the kitchen. As she did this in her mind, she counted the steps necessary to reach each destination; these small journeys she had once made without thought had suddenly become momentous.

I found myself wishing I had some physical explanation for the mornings when I lay in bed unable to make those same journeys. The depression, often accompanied by a racing heartbeat, was there in the room as soon as I woke. It was in that first sliver of consciousness, in that instant before I was aware of the light through the blinds, or of who I was. Some mornings, miraculously, it wasn't there, and I got out of bed and started the day like a normal person. But most mornings its iron bars locked down my limbs. It had a weight to it, like a mattress. I lay unmoving, and even if there were stripes of baby-blue sky and sunlight through the blinds, my mind was bathed in grey. I was flooded with the same nameless, nauseating terror that a friend who once complained about his depression had described — an unfocused sense of impending doom, as of your own death or dismemberment, made more unbearable because it was without cause. You could not say, *Well,*

I'm lying here frightened to death because I have just lost my life's savings, or *I have been diagnosed with cancer,* or *there is a stranger in the room standing over me holding an axe.* There is only your hammering heartbeat and the black curtain dropping down across your mind.

As minutes, then hours, passed, I tried to coax myself out of bed. I visualized getting up, walking to the bathroom, and washing my face. But what sounded simple was actually made up of a multitude of complex tasks. There were all the steps across the bedroom to the bathroom, first of all. Then I would have to turn on the tap, pull my hair away from my face with a hairband, and squeeze some cleanser onto my palm. I would have to massage the cleanser into my skin and wait for it to foam. Then I'd have to wash off the residue and dry my face on a towel. Already this filled me with despair. But was that the end? No, I would have to take a shower, which involved much, much more. I squeezed my eyes shut, thinking of the articles of clothing I would have to put on after the shower — tugging underpants up my legs, clasping a bra behind my back, getting dressed. Each of these rituals, which were usually performed mindlessly, appeared now to be insurmountable hurdles. The thought of rubbing deodorant under my arms wore me out. All of these personal-grooming details seemed pointless and torturously repetitive. I thought of the years ahead, of all the times I would have to wash my face, take a shower, put on deodorant, get dressed. My mind raced desperately around the thought, poking at it like a sore tooth. That first step towards the bathroom was only the first of thousands of small efforts that had to be made that day, and that one step bore in my mind the weight of all those other efforts, so it seemed I was not simply heading to the bathroom but doing a million impossible, meaningless things at once.

But you do rise. Unfortunately, the energy it has taken you to throw off the depression and swing your legs over the side of the bed — the result of hours of arguing with yourself, coaxing yourself, rationalizing with yourself, and visualizing yourself performing this singular action — has more or less spent your day's allotment of drive.

What do you have left to give to the day? I thought of work, chores, and social gatherings with equal weariness. All I longed to do was sleep; the day had barely begun, and already I was anticipating the earliest possible hour when I could sneak back to bed as though to an illicit lover. The thought of sleep was creamy, voluptuous. I ached for the moment when I could settle into my queen-sized bed under its white duvet, the pillows banked around me, and drift. I would curl up into my smallest possible self, no bigger in my mind's eye than a bean, and wait for deliverance.

Like someone who had lost a limb, the daily world had to be renavigated, discovered anew. You were no longer living in it as yourself, but as someone who was depressed. Things you had done without thinking now had to be considered with the greatest care; you had to talk yourself through every deed, you had to struggle. I held the thought of sleep in my mind like a carrot, a reward glimmering at the end of that day's obstacle path. I vowed not to succumb to the bed's soft white envelope before then; most days I managed, but when I lay down on the black leather sofa in my living room it felt like a coffin, which was curiously comforting, and I would want to sleep there, too. I wanted to do only the bare minimum to sustain life; I breathed shallowly, sensing the slowing of my heart, the blood sluggishly making its rounds through my body. I would lie there and look up at the popcorn ceiling, while the phone went unanswered and fax messages scrolled onto the floor.

It was important not to give in to the depression but impossible not to, by degrees. The newspaper, after months of struggle, was the first to go. I found I could hardly read any more. *The Globe and Mail* would take most of the day; I would start reading at breakfast and still be reading it in the middle of the afternoon. The words refused to cooperate; I stared at them perplexedly, black columns on greyish newsprint. I would read a sentence, or a paragraph, and have no idea what had just passed before my eyes. I would read an entire article, laboriously, gritting my teeth until my jaw ached, struggling to understand. But I could not concentrate. Frustrated, I would turn to *The New Yorker*, *Harper's*, a book. I could not hold anything in my mind. The words lay on the surface, skimmed across my vision, would not sink in. My mind was seething with its own drama; compulsively, it went around and around, reliving incidents in the failed relationships, scenes from years past, my childhood. The sentences on the page veered off in all directions and demanded a superhuman attention I could not provide. It seemed as if each sentence was a new thought unrelated to the previous one or the one following, and I could not stitch them together into a coherent story. My mind was so cluttered, so close to boiling over with obsessive thoughts, that I thought I could empathize with schizophrenics who hear voices — there seemed to be a similar, though not audible, clamour in my own head, above which the news of the world could not be heard.

Formulating sentences of my own was similarly arduous. John Updike, in an essay about his writing life, described approaching his desk in the morning with "a religious fear." I knew what he meant, even on the days when I was in the middle of a poem or a story and eager to work. That fear never went away, and most days it was justified — I would stare blindly at the blank page, every fifteen minutes or so typing out a clumsy line that would later find its way into the trash. I would pace the well-worn track in my carpet, play music, drink glass after glass of ice water in lieu of the cigarettes I used to smoke, open and close the refrigerator door disconsolately, make unnecessary phone calls. I thought of John Cheever who, it was rumoured, tied himself to his chair with ropes while he worked so he would be unable to rise and flee, like a sane person would do. But when I forced myself to sit for long periods in front of the typewriter my thoughts would wander, I would begin to yawn, tears of boredom would leak from the corners of my eyes, and nothing more would be accomplished than if I went out into the day, the city beyond the glass walls of my solarium.

That was what writing was like, on normal days, and in a depression this scenario simply could not be entertained. Instead, I barely set foot in my office. Answering the telephone or composing a fax message was challenging enough. The words that lived inside my head were scrambled. They had to be pulled out like taffy, carefully, to shape complete and fathomable sentences. It took all my concentration. I felt barely capable of speaking, let alone writing. Anything more complicated than a simple greeting was like crawling through miles of mud. I worried that I sounded strange to other people; to my own ears everything I said sounded stilted and slightly wrong, with an odd inflection, as if I had quite forgotten how to speak properly. I covered it up by laughing a lot and deflecting attention onto those I was speaking to by asking them so many questions about themselves that they didn't have much of a chance to interrogate me. The jangling telephone infused me with panic, but I knew I had to answer it, though the effort to make conversation was so great that I found myself perspiring. This was the key: once something was given up, it might be gone for good. If I didn't answer this phone call, didn't pay this bill, didn't do this week's laundry or go to next weekend's party, I might never do any of these things again. I knew I couldn't give in to the panic, obey that impulse. It was a haunting feeling. I thought of the agorophobe who one day obeys his fierce impulse to turn back from the errand he has set out to do, and never leaves the house again.

Before the depression — and it was like that, there was a time before and then a time after — I loved dinner parties. The conversations, the food and wine, the warm company of friends, the stimulating addition of strangers. After the depression came, dinner parties were to be endured, and I didn't always know how. I would arrive early, hoping that would compensate for the fact that I would inevitably be the first to leave. At first I drank too much, hoping to recover some sparkle or sheen, the verbal faculty and the capacity for enjoying the company of others that I had lost. For a while, alcohol presented itelf as a viable cure for depression

— it poured a bright glaze over my vision, improved my affect, restored some cheer. I would feel a rush of energy and bonhomie, my tongue would loosen and words would trip out as easily as they once used to. But, of course, the depression the next day would be that much worse, and eventually I began to limit myself to two or three drinks over the course of long dinners. Thus I would be sober — in every sense of the word. Moribund, really. In a way, this was worse. Around the table people would be rocking with laughter, gesticulating, their voices rising in volume, conversations competing with each other in noise and conviction. I strained to laugh along, weakly, in order to convince the host that I was having a good time even though I wasn't adding to the conversation. I stared at the faces around me, their mouths gaping, their eyes shiny and intoxicated, their laughter louder than jackhammers. I looked blankly at the rows of exposed teeth and gum, and it seemed I could see, with a sort of detached X-ray vision, the skulls beneath the stretched skin. That was all these people were, skeletons temporarily covered with flesh and pretense. I wanted to cover my ears with my hands. Somewhere in the multiple threads of conversation there was a story, a joke, but I could not follow it, could not catch it. Their voices assailed me from all sides in a cacophony. I let myself drift, dreaming of my white bed, my soft square of sleep. In the bathroom, away from the loud guests, I would look at myself in the mirror, where my face appeared round and puffy from too much sleep, waiting a few merciful, quiet minutes before ducking back out to the party as into a hail of bullets.

Often, someone would say something that would send me into a rage. It is said that depression is rage turned inwards, rage given no other outlet. I thought of depression as the grey side of a coin that is scarlet on its reverse. The rage was always lurking; a woman's hooting laughter in a darkened theatre would not simply irritate, it would touch off in me the entire store of built-up rage, completely unrelated to her. I would hunch in my seat, weaving an elaborate fantasy of torturing, raping, and murdering her. Someone would say something seemingly innocuous, and my blood would choke as it boiled. I would feel as if I were drowning in a sea of red; I would try to stay on the surface, but wave after wave would submerge me. I had not known anger like this since my adolescence, my childhood — the sort of rage that comes when you are accused of something you haven't done, or when a repulsive stranger is running his hands over your body. It was a child's anger, uncontainable, overwhelming. It was all I knew. I swallowed and tried to hold it back, but my heart would be racing and it would take everything not to crush the wineglass in my hand, to feel shards of glass bristling out of my flesh, or throw it against the wall and watch the pieces rain down. I practically panted with the effort of holding back, and though I never did what I wanted to do — mostly because I would suddenly have a clear and terrifying memory of my schizophrenic aunt, who when I was a child would throw dishes against the wall during dinner in an attack of rage and paranoia — I did derail a few social occasions with the anger I couldn't stop from spilling over. It shamed me, this impotent rage, this impatience with the people around me — their little habits, which I had previously barely noticed, now irritated me so much I wanted to claw their faces until they bled. How do you admit such monstrous thoughts, even to yourself? But that was the severity of it. Something that might once have been a minor irritation, a fly buzzing in another room of the house, was now nails running down a chalkboard next to my ear.

Mostly, though, I tried to pretend to have a good time and began yawning around eleven o'clock, telling everyone I had not had much sleep lately and was sorry but I was just so tired. By then I would have been agitatedly waiting for a chance to escape for the past hour. It was a kind of pain, waiting for that opportunity to leave, and then being thwarted by the inevitable stretch of time that lapsed between the first announcement of one's leave-taking, everyone's exhortations to stay, the pouring of another drink, being pulled into other conversations, the numbingly long goodbyes at the door, and the final escape. Then I would find myself running down the street, in the cold midnight air and the rain, running home.

How different is one person's tale of depression from another's? Is it often only the same story? Writing this essay, I was afraid to read the work of other people who had written in detail about their depressions — I worried that not only would the story be the same, but we would have somehow found the same language to describe it. The same phrases, the same words. How many ways are there to examine this litany of inertia,

anxiety, anger, and detachment? To describe a mental
landscape from which all pleasure has drained, leaving
it like, I imagine, the surface of the moon, pitted and
barren? How could an affliction that feels so personal
and singular, and in many ways inexpressible, actually
be shared by so many? Like those ads that appear from
time to time in the newspaper, run by some university
or research group: "Are you depressed?" and, following,
some of the symptoms. You recognize yourself, but it
seems as generic as those pamphlets in the doctor's
office asking if you are an alcoholic, and you are
because you, too, have lied about your drinking, missed
work because of it, drink because you are nervous in
social situations, etc.

Many of the people I know are depressed. They are
on Prozac, Zoloft, Wellbutrin, Paxil. Sometimes they
are also taking Xanax or Ativan, for anxiety. They drift
from one antidepressant to another, trying each on for
size, like shoes or suits of clothes. One will fit them, will
magically transform them into other people, people
better than the ones they are: happier, more confident,
with sleeker profiles and more polished personalities. I
watched one friend's scowling countenance metamor-
phose within weeks into a round smiley face after he

began taking antidepressants, as if he had taken off one mask and put on another. I did not quite know how to react; he seemed to have become someone else. Before, he was more sensitive than most people to nuances in conversations and relationships, and suffered for long periods over what he felt or didn't feel for his girlfriends or whether he had done the right thing by his friends, family, or society. He was unhappy, and had a tendency to wear his unhappiness like a badge the way many depressed people do, but I liked his ability to question deeply his motivations, to worry over emotional issues, to feel the shock of empathy. His medicated version had such a permanent smile on its face it looked like it had been drawn on with a marker. Everything seemed to skate across his surface; words and actions and emotions directed at him bounced off like coins off a bright, reflective chunk of plastic. He could not be dented.

Sometimes the mask slipped; there were brief periods when the medication didn't work, when he needed his dosage adjusted, and he was mired in darkness, his voice on the phone flattened, devoid of affect. But then he would be his superficial, happy self again, and I would watch him uncomprehendingly, I suppose glad for him, but it was as if the person I had known was gone, and this was a new person entirely, one with whom I had no connection. Now he was competent and did not waste time on the sort of self-examination that often leads to paralysis of action. His productivity increased, he seized fresh opportunities, and he began doing very well in his profession, travelling and making more money than before. He stopped worrying about whether he was capable of falling in love with anyone; he simply enjoyed his relationships and did not appear to suffer any angst over them. Now he just lived his life, and appeared to derive pleasure from it. But why did I feel, looking at his face, as if I were looking only at a surface, underneath which much of who he was had been erased?

Depression often seems to be accompanied by a certain level of narcissism. Its sufferers are always telling you how they feel, always checking the barometer of their emotional weather. They issue reports on it as they would on a matter of national significance. When I talk to my depressed acquaintances, their unhappiness becomes a claim on my attention and concern. A simple "How are you?" will elicit a detailed report on the person's recent moods and emotional states. This is the world they have come to occupy, the one they are trapped inside, and for all they know it has taken on the dimensions of the physical world itself. There is no other news, no weather or wars in another hemisphere. When you are not depressed yourself, it is a difficult state to tolerate in another. There is no visible wound to bandage, no doctor's pronouncement of a terminal illness with which to sympathize. There is only the unspooling of the grey ribbon of their days. You want to order them to pull themselves up by their bootstraps, to take a good hard look at those around them who are less fortunate and yet still manage to notice the sun shining in the sky, the first tulips pushing out of the earth. I look at the people around me who are depressed and I see people who are well educated, who have interesting jobs and professions, who are attractive and healthy, who grew up in good neighbourhoods, who have pleasant homes and loving, tolerant partners. Or maybe not all of the above, but most of it. And though their suffering is as real to them as a severed limb, it cannot help appearing to the observer like an affliction of the spoiled and wasteful, like the behaviour of an anorexic or bulimic would seem to the starving in Africa.

Their voices on the phone, disembodied, are instant indicators of their emotional states. When they are depressed, the usual highs and lows of inflection, of life and curiousity and enthusiasm, are drained away. Sometimes they cry, and then they sound like children, inconsolable.

They take their antidepressants and sometimes the magic does not work. One acquaintance of mine, who is compellingly beautiful, articulate, and creative, floods her small body with alcohol and weaves her car down the street and across the bridge in the early hours of the morning. Another friend of mine disappears into his job and his apartment for months on end, so unwilling to inflict his misery on his friends that he simply withdraws from all social activity. Perhaps his is the most gracious behaviour, but it is also the most worrisome. With another acquaintance it is easy to see when he is taking his antidepressants and when he is trying to wean himself off them — he loses or gains about fifty pounds accordingly, as his unmedicated self seeks solace in food. Other friends have adulterous sexual affairs, work obsessively, binge and throw up, take overdoses, visit therapists, or alleviate loneliness by joining one support group after another.

As a teenager, I begged my various doctors for anti-depressants, when I wasn't begging for drugs I found reliably mood-elevating or calming, such as painkillers and tranquilizers. I had no intention of taking them every day, like vitamin pills. I meant to stockpile them for a suicide attempt, and this must have been clear to those doctors, who all refused my requests. I did manage to secure a bottle of antidepressants from a john at one point, which combined with all my painkillers and sleeping pills would probably have done the job, but over the years life must have gotten better, because when I look they are no longer in my desk drawer.

I have never taken an antidepressant, and thus cannot describe — though the writer in me would like to — the physical and emotional changes, the sway and lift, the swirling sparkling grainy patterns of behaviour breaking apart and re-forming. I wonder what about me would change, and cannot imagine the world emerging from under the shadow of certain depressive behaviours — the sun coming out and a crisp slant to the architecture, everything clearly delineated, unmuddied. What would it be like to be free of those burdens, how many more hours in the day would there suddenly be to learn something new? Would my thoughts stop rotating obsessively around the tracks and grooves worn into my mind? Would I suddenly be free of whatever it is that immobilizes me, tethers me firmly to the past? It is a short leash that extends only so far as I strain towards defining a new life for myself, my own life, away from parental expectations and childhood experiences that redefine, over and over, all my relationships — from the most casual conversation with the grocery clerk to the most intimate sexual entanglement — so that it sometimes seems to me that our fate is to live out our lives replaying what hurt us, what was taken away from us or denied us when we were small, watchful, easily damaged creatures.

What has stopped me from trying antidepressants, at least as an experiment, is the fear, of course, that I will no longer be able to access the part of myself that writes, that is in some way fuelled by all the afflictions that otherwise make me miserable as a person. For it is in the compulsions, the obsessions, the seemingly fathomless emotional experiences, that some of that writing is born. It is in that ability to go so deeply into a subject that it is like dropping down a hole into the heart of the known world. When I have tentatively expressed this concern, afraid of its possible pretence — the underlying naive belief that writers and poets have to suffer for their art, that if Prozac had existed back then there would not have been a Charles Baudelaire or a Sylvia Plath — people I know have assured me that if anything their medication has made them more productive at work, because they are no longer mired in their depressions, or at least spend less time in that state. They are no longer held back by the voices in their heads that tell them they can't succeed, they can't try anything new, they'll only fail or make fools of themselves, so why bother going on that holiday with your lover, or applying for that job, or joining a class and learning how to ballroom dance or kick-box? But none of these people writes creatively. So while I am convinced that I might have a happier, more well-rounded life that I would like, one in which I am not held back by my fears and old behaviours, one in which I might well write many more articles per year than I would in my depressed, worried, neurotic state, I wonder whether the poems would come. The stories? The words that I wrench from that personal, tangled place?

Would I spend as much time in the state a friend's father described as "circling" — all those activities with which one fills the hours before one finally sits down at the desk and writes? The wall of resistance to my work is some days so strong that by the time I do sit down to work I feel I've returned from a battlefield and deserve rest and consolation, not another war. My friends who work at home commiserate with me over our various forms of avoidance, while the precious minutes and then hours tick past as we talk, make coffee or tea, and talk some more. I think in frustration of the well-dressed lawyers in their firms downtown, the business people and the stockbrokers, every minute counted and billed out, the way they burn through their work, while here I am in my bathrobe, desperately holding at bay the hour when I can no longer procrastinate and must finally work. Sometimes that hour does not come until the evening, when everyone else is returning home, trudging down the street in the twilight carrying a briefcase and drycleaning, looking forward to a hot dinner and an evening of television. Some days the depression is so severe that a single errand seems like a day's work, and the smallest thing is in fact the heaviest lifting any person can be asked to do. Some days the exhaustion is such that even television seems too intellectually challenging, and the only programs that can be endured are reruns of the after-school shows meant for teenagers. Every planned or spontaneous event, either work-related or social, is like running a marathon for which you have never trained. Panic buzzes around the edges of your otherwise sluggish consciousness. You lie about having other things to do, other places to go, so friends won't wonder or worry when you turn down their invitations. But all you want to do — long for it, yearn for it with a kind of passion — is to be alone, lying on the sofa, listening to the slow, subterranean thump of your heartbeat, while the light dims in the framed window. Could a mere pill dissolve all that in an instant? Would all those barriers simply evaporate, so that I could walk to my desk early in the morning not through a quagmire of heavy mud and quicksand, but through shining air?

"I was born depressed," a man I went out with used to say. His pale eyes veered away from mine, focusing on his depthless inner misery; when they met my gaze again, the irises looked dull in the light from the window. It was worst in the mornings; he would wake with his forehead furrowed, his hand pressed over his eyes, as if to ward off the world encroaching on his consciousness. I came to dread these morning moods, turning towards him nervously as he delivered his emotional weather forecast. It would colour the events of the day ahead as reliably as the forecast on the radio. "I feel *so* depressed," he would groan, reluctantly uncovering his eyes and staring up at the ceiling. "I woke up with my heart racing, thinking, 'What's the point? What does anything matter, anyway?'"

Early on in our relationship I felt a surge of sympathy; I would wrap my arms around his inert figure, trying to transfer some of my warmth to him. I thought I could rouse him from his dark place, with my attentions and the sunlight streaming in through the open blinds. I teased, cajoled, kissed, and caressed. I would have stood on my head or juggled circus balls if that would have helped. As months passed, my sympathy eroded first into impatience and then into something close to anger. His depression was as formless and engulfing as a fog, and impossible to avoid. When I lay against him I could almost feel it creeping into me. I began to resent, like a jealous lover, what he held closest to his heart: his own depression. He was locked into it and I did not have the key or the combination.

When he looked at me his gaze was empty, as though I were not a person but a space. I thought about how strong you would have to be, to survive being looked at in that way without anger and resentment flooding through you, without feeling like a child who is persistently ignored and will soon burst into a tantrum. And again it seemed I felt most sorry for the people around the depressed person — the friends and relatives who watched, tried to be patient, tried to help and indulge and quietly counsel, but many of whom surely reached a point where they wanted to drag the person upright, demand that their wills return to their limp bodies and again assume control over their lives, because they were adults, not helpless, not visibly sick, not children. I have always had that uncomprehending impatience with and vague dislike of people I know who are depressed; at times I want to hit them. I felt the same way towards myself when I was depressed, but magnified — what was left of the sensate part of me shouted at me from a great distance, in contempt and loathing, in huge, swelling impatience. *Pull yourself together! I'll give you something to cry about!* Depressed people are so tiresome, dispiriting. It is awful to see the life of someone you know and care for unwind in a great ribbon of waste in front of you, unappreciated, unobserved even, to see them huddled in a dingy corner of the landscape of opportunity and promise that they cannot see, let alone navigate. It is even more awful when it is your own life, and the guilt at the static place in which you have found yourself is itself crippling, immobilizing. How greatly taxed are those whose lives revolve around the depressed person's. How hard it is to love those who are depressed without suffering some injury to yourself, without losing yourself, dropping down into their black pit, sucked into their vortex of need.

"Life is not a worth," my psychiatrist insisted one day when, after months of depression, I ventured the opinion that life was not worth living. His light-filled office was the square of space I could fill with words I could not speak elsewhere; even here they sounded whining and weak to my own ears, a steady drone of misery and complaint. I prided myself on my refusal to share my depression with my acquaintances the way so many depressed people do, seeking some fleeting relief from the unending drabness of their inner worlds in another's brief, bright gaze of compassion or attention. This was what made it possible, to share it here, to unlatch the spring on Pandora's box and let the storm of winged evils swarm out. "Life is not a value, it's not about whether it's worth living."

He talked, as he sometimes did, about his admiration for a certain "nobility of spirit," which I clearly saw I lacked. I felt ashamed of my constant ill humour, but once unstoppered it poured out like black bile, like the fluids that physicians in ancient times drew out of the body to alleviate melancholia. What I wanted to say, what was constantly felt, was "What's the point?" This was what I had come to feel about every endeavour, yet I disliked my depressed friends when they said it themselves. I could hear their voices — by turns angry and childish and demanding. It was their motto, their tiresome refrain: "What's the point?" As though it were owed to them that someone, somewhere, should be held accountable, should be made to stand up and explain to them the point of life and of activity inside that life, the point of getting up in the morning, going to work, eating three meals, and not committing suicide before sundown. What if there was no point, no right to demand one? What if nobility of spirit was simply to go on, one day after the next, without losing hope, without falling into despair?

I don't know if there is any way of describing one's experience with depression that isn't inherently self-involved. Now that depression has been recognized as an illness, now that some of the shame cloaking it has fallen away, do we instead err on the side of indulging it, coddling it, always bending a sympathetic ear to the tiresome song of its sufferers for fear of appearing insensitive? I still want to believe it can be conquered by mind over matter, even on those days when I feel a palpable sickening of the spirit, when I can feel my own mind turning again towards the darkness. I want to believe that depression is no more concrete than a shadow, a ghost in the attic. A mirage that can be blinked away, when the sun shines hard upon it and it vanishes like a veil of dust, and there is nothing left but all else that remains — the room, the light, the objects in the world.

FATHER FIGURES

DISTANCE, FOR ME, kindles desire. When I was growing up it was my crushes on teachers that preoccupied me, not the freckle-faced boy's fumbling kiss behind the bushes at recess. Not what was close and possible. It was these older men with their mysterious lives whom I invested with the power of protecting me.

It has always been this way, and sometimes I think it always will be. At almost any given time I will have a crush on a man who is somehow impossible. The word "crush" is appropriate, because the feeling is entirely adolescent in its short-lived intensity. The object of my distant affections is likely someone I have met only a few times, someone who displays no interest in me. He has no inkling of the feelings I have for him; quite possibly he would be startled and embarrassed if he knew. I never express my interest, since if he responded that would instantly end my infatuation.

If he is married, he will have shown himself to be the sort of married man who has affairs, and who is therefore untrustworthy. If he isn't married, his availability alone would send me running. Besides, if I actually got to know him better I would have to acknowledge that his real personality bears no resemblance to the inordinately loving and attentive one I had given him in my thoughts.

Although these crushes are not without some of the heartache of unrequited love, I do enjoy them, in a way. They are innocent, uncomplicated by sex, or spending the night, or the daily challenges of a relationship. They are curiously pure; my imagination rarely indulges in anything more intimate than kissing and cuddling. As I write this, I am nursing a crush on a middle-aged married man. He is successful and driven, obsessed with his work; he wears conservative suits and has the face of someone's rich uncle. I have met him twice and will probably never see him again. This is fine by me, since I try so hard to conceal my interest that I am awkward and speechless around him. I would welcome his presence in my life, but the sensations he stirs in me make friendship impossible. At the same time, only by getting to know him better, understanding who he is independent of my fantasy, could I put him into human perspective and end my infatuation.

When I look back over the past decade, I am dismayed by how often desire, or even the perceived threat of desire — a man's or my own — has prevented the inclusion in my life of some interesting, even brilliant men. A wife's groundless jealousy in situations where no attraction exists, a man's confessed infatuation, a drunken kiss one regrettable night — each is enough to create a permanent rift.

Desire, for me, is often strangely divorced from sex. What I most desire — an entrance into another's life, the sudden flare of emotional contact, intellectual stimulation — is not compelled by a sexual motive. But this sort of desire can be as powerful an urge as sex. I once had an intense emotional connection with a married man that never involved sex, yet it so threatened his wife that it contributed to the end of their marriage. How could she believe that the most risqué fantasy I had was that I might put my head on his shoulder, breathe in his comforting, paternal smell, and go to sleep? How could she believe that the driving force of my life has been to find a man who would look at me as though I were his daughter?

My father adored me when I was a child. It appeared I was the centre of his universe; when we played together my reflection danced in the lenses of his glasses, as if I were all that filled his vision. I loved him passionately and would spend long nights agonizing about losing him — he would be attacked on his way home from work, he would sicken and die, my mother would force him to leave. His safety was paramount in my mind, so that my mother's interference in the capsule of our love was not merely an inconvenience to me but a real threat — when he finished my bedtime story and proceeded down the hall to the bedroom he shared with her, I would lie awake gripped with fear, certain that she was waiting in the darkness to injure him.

To lose my father would be to lose not only love and attention but the shield between myself and my mother, whom I saw as a frightening force, prone to unpredictable rages and a need for humiliating dominance over me. I prayed nightly for his safety; he survived intact, but when I was nine years old my mother gave birth to another baby girl, and his attention flickered away from me. Then he lost his job, and our lives changed. He entered the world of his own misery, trudging home day after day from job interviews that led nowhere. He would disappear into the basement to prepare more resumés and to do the contract work that provided our meagre income. My mother belittled him for being unemployed, and her anxiety over our financial future aggravated her compulsive behaviour. Desperate to escape my mother's control, murderously jealous of my new sibling, bewildered by the withdrawal of my father's affection, I became obsessed with writing and the fantasy life it afforded. At school I was an outcast, and the combination of my classmates' merciless teasing and my unhappiness at home meant I spent most nights praying that I would die in my sleep. To comfort myself, I began bingeing secretly, which led to constant mockery of my body from my mother and an embarrassed averting of my father's gaze from my growing chubbiness. Depressed, nearly suicidal, I would sit in my room gorging on hoarded food while my parents went shopping on weekends. It seemed to me then that everything had already been lost.

At fourteen, I ran away from the life I could no longer endure. I left the father I could no longer look at without pain clouding my vision, and stood on street corners so other fathers could pay attention to me for as long as it took to give them an orgasm. Prostitution was my introduction to sex; inevitably, it confused my understanding of desire and inhibited my interest in my own sexuality. I learned to regard desire as something that resided, raging, only in men. Often the sex I had with clients was so repugnant and physically uncomfortable that I swallowed painkillers beforehand, in order to feel as little as possible. It took years to emerge from that period of my life, with all its self-destructive behaviour, and when I did I actually thought I might never have sex again, though its darker permutations fascinated me as a writer. Sex lent itself so readily to literary explorations of power, of loyalty and its absence, of boundaries tested.

I was amazed when people would ask me questions like, "Just between us, didn't you *enjoy* it when you were hooking?" How could they be so ignorant, particularly the women? But these were women who had had mostly positive sexual experiences, who praised the physical sensation of intercourse. They didn't seem to know what it was like to be so unwilling that it was painful to have a stranger's penis inside you, or to be so numb and detached that you felt absolutely nothing. They couldn't comprehend it because they hadn't lived it, just as when I was a teenager I couldn't understand why anyone would ever have sex unless she was being paid for it.

But when I was twenty years old I fell desperately in love with a married man who lived in another city, and for several years I drowned in the certainty that I had met the one person meant for me. He was a prominent executive, polished and urbane; privately, he was tormented. When we met, on a night during which rain ran into the gutters, I was stricken — the blaze of his eyes as we sat next to each other at the restaurant, his skin as smooth as white stone. I was mesmerized by him in a way I never thought possible. Later he said that when he drove home that night, thinking about me, he was shaking.

Our "affair" consisted of hotel room fumblings that never culminated in intercourse, and long conversations during which he would cry because he wanted to be with me but could not bear to end his marriage. He was really the first person I met that I wanted to be with, the first man with whom I was able to equate sex and love, physical desire and emotional desire. His childhood poverty, his father's physical abuse, and his self-made success had developed a wariness in him that mirrored my own, and a similar ability to make swift assessments of people's motivations. It took years for the pain of our impossible relationship to subside. Even after it became clear that he would never leave his wife, and that we must not continue seeing each other, I could not imagine going on dates or sleeping with other men. I hated myself, thought that if I were more attractive or confident he would have stayed with me. I know he is still living with his glamorous blonde wife. The gold band gleams on his finger. Even now, after a few drinks with friends, I sometimes like to say that if he were to walk in the door today and ask me to marry him, I would. Such is the effect, I suppose, of that first instance of looking at someone and wanting him entirely: his skin, his scent, his power, and his vulnerability. It was the first time I had seen physical beauty in a man, the first time I had longed for someone with all my heart.

The entanglement with this man made me miserable. At times I thought I was losing my mind. There is a history of schizophrenia on my mother's side of the family — as a child, I worried that every imaginative thought I had, every period of depression or anxiety, heralded the advent of my own psychosis — and I grew up watching an aunt throw dishes against the wall during dinner, or start to scream because she saw men's faces in the mirror ogling her when she stepped out of the shower. Periodically she would wander the streets, and we would get late-night phone calls from the psychiatric ward informing us that she had been brought in by ambulance. When we visited her in the hospital she shuffled towards us in her fluffy slippers, looking small and embarrassed, apologizing to my parents for having again brought shame upon our family. My relatives blamed her craziness on the scourge of unrequited love. It was said that the psychotic episodes began when she fell obsessively in love with her boss, who was married and had no interest in her. The sorrow of this had snapped something in her brain. It was a romantic notion without sound medical support, but during the worst periods of my own obsession, when there was clearly no chance for this man and me, it didn't appear so implausible. I never thought I could be so consumed by another person.

Now, I find it remarkable and a bit dismaying how rare
it is for me to desire someone beyond a mild, entertain-
ing crush. I meet men of all ages who I like and admire,
whose intellect and wit impress me, but I feel absolutely
no attraction to them. I have gone on dates with men
who fit the picture of what I typically find appealing,
but who fail to provide the least spark or surge of feeling. What is that thing that catches at your heart, seizes
you, shakes you? What are the chemical reactions over
which we have no command? I have many male friends
and enjoy the company of men, but these relationships
are platonic. I don't understand people whose friend-
ships turn into sexual affairs, or vice versa; for me there
is a strong line between a friendship and a sexual relationship. I regard it as almost morally wrong to confuse
the two. My male friends talk to me openly about their
romantic involvements with women; if I were one of
those women, they would cease to be so honest. I prize
honesty, and despise the evasiveness and lies that sexual
relationships seem to thrive on.

I wish I could write about plain, simple, lusty desire,
the allure of another's heat and physical body, uncomplicated by thought or rationale. I have felt that sort of

desire, fleetingly, only two or three times in my life, for men who otherwise did not interest me. It confounded and terrified me, and I did everything possible to protect myself from it. It took away the control I was typically able to maintain around men. Usually the men I find myself drawn to are not physically attractive — they tend to be establishment figures, middle-aged or older, grey-haired and intellectually intimidating. They hold positions of some power in society. They may be paunchy or wrinkled, stooped or arthritic. They may have physical characteristics that actually repel me. But I find their keen insight, their paternal regard compelling; it's how observant they are, how protective they are capable of being that interests me. They possess qualities that are desirable to me, yet they are unable to weaken me with lust.

When I was a child my parents instilled in me the belief that because I am Chinese, and they are immigrants, I would always be inferior to other Canadians; I would have to work twice as hard, be twice as respectable, just to be accepted by this society. Their beliefs were reinforced by the occasional, always shocking, racial taunt in the schoolyard, on the bus, from a stranger passing on the street. A powerful mix of longing and shame roiled in me. I always felt I was an outsider, pressing my face against the glass, yearning to join those people fortunate enough to be in the light and the warmth inside. Perhaps that is partly why I was drawn from the beginning to men whose lives appeared unblemished and enviable on the surface; I wanted to be accepted by them, to find myself safe inside their houses.

I don't think I am capable of feeling desire without a complex of emotions and justifications — and that, some men might say, is just what is so unfair about the difference between women and men. For many women, it seems, and certainly for me, pure physical desire can lie dormant for long periods of time, chased underground by anything from a traumatic end to a relationship to problems at work. A female friend once told me that in the years between relationships her sexual desire dwindled "to something the size of a pea, tucked way, way back in a corner of my mind." Yet when she is in a relationship her sexual urge is as alive as that of any man she is with.

I find myself writing this essay during a rather bleak period of my life. Desire is dim, pushed down and away.

When I was twenty-four I finally ventured into another relationship, with an older writer. I have never been drawn to writers, since there is no mystery for me in what they do, no entry to an unknown world such as a man in a different occupation would provide. But this man seemed harmless, and unintimidated by my past. It ended badly, with him suing me over an article I wrote about our relationship. In writing that article I had been hoping to make sense of my time with him, redeem something that felt merely painful and wasted. But for a year and a half the lawsuit continued to tie us together when I wanted to move forward in my life. I joked with friends that the situation taught me all about marriage and divorce, without me having to actually go through either.

I try to view the litigation as a learning experience, but I worry that it will leave a stain as permanent as the one left behind by years of prostitution. This man, thirty-six years older than I, had come closer than anyone to mirroring my relationship with my father; I saw him as a protector, and the lawsuit devastated me.

An acquaintance of mine, a stylish woman in her forties with a good career, was financially ruined by her divorce from a high-flying entrepreneur years ago. She remains flirtatious with men, almost girlish, but she is hard-hearted now. She rarely dates, and she speaks of men in a calculating way, in terms of what they can give her. She recognizes her need for sex as a nuisance that must be taken care of now and then; once or twice a year she goes on holiday, drinks too much and ends up in bed with a stranger, kicking him out the next morning without giving him her real name or her phone number. She refers to sex as an "animal" urge that must be satisfied occasionally, but she's not likely to risk her heart again.

Some days I understand the way she feels, and wonder if that is what is in store for me. Other days I long for attachment, for the bond I see between couples holding hands as they walk down the street or nestling against each other in restaurant banquettes. As a writer, I crave solitude and cling to my earned independence. I have always been fascinated by marriage, by what binds people together, but cannot seem to imagine it for myself. For a long time I wanted to believe that there was only one person in the world for me, or for that matter for anyone — that love was singular and unmistakable and once-in-a-lifetime. I didn't understand how a feeling as powerful as love could change to hatred or indifference. I remember reading about a prominent businessman who, during his rancorous divorce, yelled into his wife's answering machine, "I promise God I will destroy you!" How do you go from wanting with everything in your heart to be good to the person you have chosen to love, to that?

I want to trust in the permanence of love, to believe that desire can last. But the reality is that I seem incapable of forming a relationship based on mutuality. I look at my friends in their thirties, married to people their own age, starting a life together with a house and a mortgage and two jobs and thoughts of children. I see that they truly have a partnership, but that is the last thing I want for myself. The thought of sharing my life as an equal with another person almost repulses me. It doesn't coincide with my fantasy of finding a father figure, something that goes right through all the structures of my being.

So, at twenty-seven, I find myself back in my psychiatrist's office. He is the safest person I know. He looked after me during my adolescence; this past year, as an adult, I started seeing him again. In some respects I never left him; he has always inhabited me, my deepest thoughts, my dreams. I know a little more about him now than I did before, yet the distance is still there, the stern gulf between doctor and patient. But we sometimes banter and laugh, and I suppose that someone listening to us would think we sound like two people who have known each other for a long time, which we have. I occasionally desire him, in a wistful sort of way. I imagine how safe I would feel in his arms, and that this time I would not be wrong. He is roundish, with a kind, genial face. Once, when he spoke of his wife of more than thirty years, he said, "Her grace can stop a room." His eyes softened, and I thought then that what they had was what I wanted, after all.

I often arrive early for our sessions, so I can experience the tense pleasure of waiting for him at the top of the staircase as I used to wait for my father to return from work, clamouring to be the first to greet him, the smell and the scratch of his tweed jacket against my face. Then, at the bottom of the stairs I see the doctor's thick, cherubic body as he enters the building, and I am flooded with the same relief — he has not come to harm, he has not forgotten me. I see the preoccupied look on his face, his smile when I call down to him. The keys jangle in his hand as he pounds up the stairs, unlocks the door, lets me in.

There are days I long to climb into his lap, curl up there like a child or a kitten, and indeed when I can't sleep I sometimes picture myself that way, as small as a doll in his lap. But what makes this desire possible is the necessary distance between us. I know I will never sit in his lap, that he will never threaten or destroy me by reaching out for me. Without the mercurial tides of sexual involvement, desire can sometimes be as uncomplicated as this — wanting to feel safe, held in another's gaze and attention, in that constant and unchanging light.

AN INSATIABLE
EMPTINESS

I NO LONGER CLEARLY remember the first time I forced myself to throw up. What I do remember is how inexpert I was and how long it took before I succeeded in actually vomiting instead of just gagging and retching. I began by sticking my finger down my throat and wiggling it around, but this produced few results; it wasn't until articles about bulimia appeared in women's magazines that I finally thought to use the handle of a toothbrush instead of my forefinger. It became easy after that.

In my mid-teens, I was too young to believe I was anything but immortal. It didn't occur to me that what I was doing was dangerous — instead, it seemed a smart and practical way of coping with things. I went through months of throwing up once or twice a day, then brief periods when I did not throw up at all, when I seemed to have broken the pattern. Surely this meant

I was in control. But by the time I was eighteen, the months of not throwing up had diminished to weeks, and when I was vomiting I was doing it four, five, six times a day. I had become addicted to the sensation. It was no longer a penance I had to perform after eating, but the reward at the end of a binge. I loved the feeling I had after purging, of being clean and shiny inside like a scrubbed machine, superhuman. I would rise from the bathroom floor, splash my face with cold water, vigorously brush the acid from my mouth. I would wipe off the vomit that had spattered my arms and feel as energized as someone who had just woken from a nap or returned from an invigorating jog around the block. I felt as if everything disgusting inside me had been displaced so that it was now outside myself. Not only all the food I had eaten, but my entire past.

No one could tell me to stop, not even my friends who eventually knew what I was doing. They could not control this part of my life. This was mine alone — the chemical flower smell of the blue water in the toilet, the vomit that shot out as a burning liquid, drenching the sides of the bowl. After a session in the bathroom, a certain emptiness would sing inside me, a sensation of having become a cage of bones with air rushing through it. I craved this feeling so much that I no longer cared what I had to eat in order to vomit — I would cram clusters of bananas into my mouth, or tubs of ice cream that lurched back up my throat in a thin and startlingly sweet projectile.

When I left the bathroom, I felt like someone who had achieved a great thing — climbed a mountain, written a book — and survived. I was overweight by only ten pounds or so, but when I looked in the mirror all I saw was buttery flesh covering my body. My stomach had become swollen and globular from the gorging and purging; I had earned it, just as other women earn washboard stomachs and lean waists from hours of crunches at the gym.

As a child I had been thin and healthy, with a flat belly and limbs that turned brown in the summer. I had my first period when I was eleven, and for the next several years the blood welled out of me in thick, rust-coloured gouts that no tampons or pads could contain. My body had somehow become a vessel filled with secret, terrible workings, and I longed to make it translucent, pared-down, clean as a whistle. But the blood spread in the shapes of clouds on my skirts and pants, for ten or twelve days each month, and my hips and breasts pressed outwards. I hated what was happening to my body, once so straight and uninflected. I attracted the attention of one of my parents' friends, who stared at the fuzzy dark crook at the top of my thighs when I sat cross-legged in front of him, who asked me to perform somersaults and splits while his thick lips hung open with desire. My own father grew awkward around me, refusing to touch me or meet my eyes, driven away by this growing body that forced him out like a giant balloon expanding inside a small room. I was in despair. I wanted to trick my body back into childhood by starving it, but I was hungry all the time; I craved food during the week prior to my traumatic menstral periods. Sometimes I would consume an entire bag of shortbread cookies or three chocolate bars; the sugar and fat would induce a heavy, mucousy lethargy.

My breasts continued to develop, horrifying my mother, who frequently made me undress in front of her so she could ridicule them. Her actions convinced me that there was something wrong with my body. She decided to put the whole family on a diet, serving small portions of steamed fish and vegetables, chicken with the skin removed. I would sit at the dinner table, staring down at my plate with tears in my eyes, grief forming a hot, choking knot in my throat. I would watch my father slowly raise his chopsticks to his mouth while my eagle-eyed mother watched me triumphantly, eating only half of what was on her plate in order to set an example.

Still, I began to put on weight, growing chubby beneath sweatshirts and loose jeans. I stole chocolates from the drugstore, bought greasy bags of day-old cookies from the bakery, consumed candies in a blind rush on the mile-long walk home from school. I crammed myself with food, yet I hated food: its veils of grease, its sauces like paste. I hated its fragility in my hands, could not bear the delicacy of pastry. But once I started eating, I could not stop, and after I gave in I would again have to cope with the horrible feeling of satiation — a feeling so uncomfortable and infused with guilt it threatened to annihilate me.

I hated the unaccustomed thickness of my body, yet I took a secret, perverse pride in the space I was filling up, the air I was pushing aside in the family home in order to make room for myself. I looked in scorn upon my mother, who wore tiny pink sweaters with pearl buttons, size XS. Her legs were like bleached sticks, the skin white and crêpey; her hipbones jutted visibly beneath her skirts, and she reminded me of a starving cow, its ribs and hips holding up the a of skin. At thirteen, I had grown to match my father's weight. But at 135 pounds he was small for a man, his arms straight, the biceps undefined. He was weak, useless in the battle that had sprung up between my mother and myself. He would not protect me, he took no sides in the daily tug-of-war for power. He merely absented himself, took the coward's way out. For this, I knew, one day I would make him suffer.

I thought that if I were to physically fight my mother I could break her dry arms like twigs. I could twist her skeleton between my hands; I could sit on her and suffocate her. But it never came to that. Instead, with each pound I gained, my mother became more controlling. I felt that there was only one thing my mother could not take away from me: my body. She was trying, of course, with her diets and carefully calibrated meals and calorie counters set up around the kitchen. She wanted to watch me day and night, but in this she inevitably encountered frustration and failure: she could not see the junk food I snuck between meals and hid between textbooks and in my locker at school.

And it was driving her crazy, I began to realize. She turned to the only thing she could control twenty-four hours a day: her own body. For every pound I gained, it seemed that she lost one. In grade nine, when I came home from school I found her doing jumping jacks and skipping rope in the living room, or following an aerobics show on television. She ate next to nothing, complaining that I was doing enough eating for both of us. Her eyes grew large in her face, and her hair began to fall out in swirls that clogged the drains in the sink and the shower. When I stood up from the table and looked down at my mother's skull, I could see the wide, white swathe of the part in her hair.

For a while, my father insisted that she eat more, but he soon gave up and came home later and later, avoiding the dinner hour, fraught as it was with agonizing tension: my mother staring at me with fascination as I ate, her eyes transfixed. I thought I could no longer stand it; I was as guilty as a murderer with every bite. At night, I lay in my room contemplating suicide and listening to the footsteps of my father pacing in his study, perhaps waiting for his wife to fall asleep before daring to enter their bedroom. When I trespassed there, I saw pink walls, pink curtains, a pink throw on the queen-sized bed. The bedroom faced south, and all day the sun shone relentlessly through the gauze curtains, revealing motes of dust in the air. When I opened the dresser drawers, I found beautiful, tiny clothes, beaded and jewelled, carefully folded and wrapped in plastic, as if their owner had already died. I knew these clothes would never again be worn by my mother, and that I would never be small enough to wear them. I knew this was a source of bitterness in my mother's life — she could not pass herself on to me; she could not live her life again through me. In order to survive, I would have to deny my mother this second life and claim my own.

In the ensuite bathroom I found orange lipsticks dried to hard, waxy nubs, cakes of powder that crumbled at a touch, an old tube of KY jelly squeezed from the bottom like toothpaste. All of it seemed a shrine to my mother's glamorous past. She had been a beauty in her youth, with thick hair that had hung down to her waist, so much hair it was almost impossible to bind into ponytails. She had had pale skin and pink cheeks like apple blossoms, and she had worn short skirts and high heels to work.

⟡

What my mother didn't know was that I was already beginning to incorporate her inside me. She didn't know that she was winning, and that for the rest of my life I would contain aspects of her. I would grow up to wear contact lenses and put a wave in my hair; I would admire myself in mirrors and spend small fortunes on clothes and cosmetics. Beneath this evidence of self-esteem, though, I would learn to cultivate a parallel self-hatred: my thoughts would repeat themselves obsessively; I would become compulsive in my behaviour; I would avoid other women because I was afraid they would try to control me like my mother had; and I would live at the mercy of my emotions, the endless sour stream of hatred that poured out of my mouth when I bent over the toilet.

The last time I saw my parents, when I was seventeen and they were in their fifties, my father seemed bewildered by what had happened to our family. My mother had become a confused, agitated woman who plucked ceaselessly at the strap of her purse with an anguished tic. She had become powerless to control me, this piece of herself that had separated from her. She had lost me in her attempt to keep me forever.

I was twenty when I began to lose my feeling of immortality. I thought my body would regenerate itself in time, that once again everything would be new and resilient. But it only got worse. My body began showing signs of wear — my throat constantly ached from throwing up, and when I opened my mouth I saw in the mirror a red, inflamed pendulum dangling behind rows of teeth softened and eroded by acid. My teeth, once so white — the sort of teeth parents thank God for; the sort of teeth a man meeting me for the first time would walk away remembering — had become pitted and yellow, the back ones worn down to shrunken saddles. When I looked in the mirror, they were as translucent as X-rays, made, it seemed, of water and putty. I began to brush more vigorously after each purge, not knowing then that I was accelerating the process of decay, scrubbing my teeth with my own stomach acid.

I waited for the day when I would throw up blood. Already I could taste it at the back of my throat, inching farther upwards with each heartbeat. Now after vomiting, I would rise shakily from my knees, gripping the edge of the counter for balance, my heart knocking wildly in my chest. A column of flame speared me from my stomach to my throat — my esophagus was a two-edged blade in my chest, a tunnel set on fire, a steel pole thrust through me.

Now when I threw up, I reeled from the pain. I was not throwing up half-digested food, as I had for years, but what felt like whole objects — plastic balls, pieces of Lego, nuts and bolts that tore at me as they came out of my body. Afterwards, my stomach would hurt so much that for the rest of the evening any sustenance I sought would have to be the sort given to a convalescent or a starvation victim: thin porridge, vegetable soup, herbal tea.

I no longer thought of myself as a girl or a woman. I felt no sexual desire. I was an "it," a conduit for a constant stream of ugliness that had to pass through in order for me to stay pure.

In some dim part of me, I knew that when I left my apartment, other people did not see me as I saw myself. They did not recoil from me in horror, as I expected. Intellectually, I knew I was a reasonably attractive young woman, like so many young women in the city, neither fat nor thin. But I felt somehow grotesque and abnormal. Strangers knew nothing of my secret; friends were helpless; my dentist would only shake his head over my open mouth and tap his pencil along my teeth to track the path of corrosion the vomit had left in its wake.

Once, in a determined moment, I called the Eating Disorders Clinic at St. Paul's Hospital, but the waiting list meant I would not get in for a year. At that time, a year seemed forever, so I did not add my name to the list. Surely in a year's time everything would have changed, resolved itself. Twelve months later I called again, but by this time the list was even longer, and again I did not add my name to it.

I was finally able to bring the bulimia under control when I was twenty-two. This happened not because of willpower or therapy or something so banal as an increased sense of self-esteem. It happened because the pain from throwing up rendered the pleasure slight by comparison. It happened when my softened teeth cringed at every mouthful and when I woke several times each night with cramps wracking my stomach from one side of my waist to the other. It happened when I arrived at the point where I could no longer feel my feet. Months later, when I went to the doctor, he would diagnose it as an electrolyte imbalance caused by vomiting up so many vitamins and minerals. But for a long time, I didn't know what it was, and it frightened me — sometimes when I stood up, I nearly fell over. My feet were cold and clammy, disconnected from the rest of my body. Once in a while they flared suddenly to life, a constellation of pins and needles, so that I could not bear to press my soles to the floor. When I tried to go to the bathroom in the middle of the night, I felt in the underwater light of that hour as if I had transformed into the fairy-tale mermaid who had chosen her lover over the sea: with each step, I landed on knife points.

By then I had also developed a hiatus hernia — a portion of my stomach protruded through my esophagus — and my teeth had become so compromised that one day one of them simply disintegrated under pressure.

"Your tooth isn't going to grow back," the dentist said flatly, and it was then I understood for the first time that my body did not possess some secret store of replacement parts, that physical damage, like its psychological counterpart, left marks that could remain for a lifetime.

On the rare occasions that I forced myself to throw up in the years that followed, it felt like internal surgery. Grief, love, rage, pain — all of it came pouring out. Yet afterwards it was still there inside me. After years of vomiting, I had not purged myself of any of the things that were making me sick.

THE OBSERVING EGO

WHEN DID IT START, this obsession, this moral compass turning and fixing in this singular direction? I remember making a pact when I was nine years old, during all those hours I lay awake in bed, with the larger presence I felt around me in the darkness. I called him my writing god. Religion was nonexistent in our household, dismissed as a waste of time by my practical parents, and indeed the books that my Catholic aunts passed to me, with their rather graphic illustrations that produced a curious tickle of titillation, did not interest me more than any other book of fairy tales or myths. Yet there was my writing god. I knit him out of the darkness in my bedroom, slowly, over many nights, so that it seemed he had always been there. I can't remember a time when he wasn't, just as I can't remember a time when I wasn't watching and recording. He belonged only to me, and the deal I made with him was that as long as he looked after my writing — helped me be a better writer, helped me publish and live my life as a writer — I would never ask him for anything else. The rest of my life could dissolve into heartbreaks and catastrophes, into a litany of losses, but as long as he made sure I was still writing and publishing, he was doing his job and I had no right to ask him for help in any other area.

As a child I thought every writer had such a deity, and I still remember the shock I felt reading about authors' deaths in the newspaper, the unfinished books they had left behind. If they had been working on manuscripts, how could they succumb to mortal illness or accident? It was their duty to finish those books, it was why they had been put on this earth; they were no more than vehicles for those stories, and their writing gods should have seen that they lived — however miserably — to carry out their work. I believed that as long as I was working on a poem, a story, a book — over two summers, when I was nine and ten, I wrote two full-length novels, long lost — I could not die. It is only now, looking back, that I think I must have been aware of my mortality and afraid of it, and that my writing god was a way of dealing with that fear. I remember walking dreamily through the neighbourhood on blazing summer afternoons, under the leafy chestnut trees, when other girls must have been playing together or trying on makeup or flirting with boys, thinking about my stories as I crossed the street. The secret I carried like a golden egg inside me was that I could step in front of traffic and remain uninjured, because I was producing a work of importance. It sounds embarrassingly egotistical now, but in a way it was not. I did not think I was more special or deserving than anyone else. It was simply that I was a kind of vessel, carrying an invaluable cargo that I had to deliver at any cost. I wonder if that part of my childhood is common to people who decide at a young age what they are meant to do with the rest of their lives, if they all have that lacuna when they feel in possession of a great thing, before they come to resent it or discover it is covered in gilt rather than gold.

The odd thing is, I still talk to my writing god. When I look up from the page, he is there. Sometimes, in a burst of enthusiasm, when I settle upon a shining line after days of wrestling in the mud, I thank him aloud, as I have always done. Then I feel complete, as if I have found my other half, the twin with whom I was meant to spend eternity, the one from whom I was parted because of mankind's hubris. But I rarely pray to him, as I used to spend hours doing; the things I want now are no longer under his jurisdiction. It is jolting to discover that I rarely want to pray for inspiration, even when the muse hides for months behind a cloud. Instead I speak to him sternly, demanding an end to our bargain. I will exchange all the written words left in my lifetime, hand them over in a bursting sack, if he will give me the other thing I currently want. But I always know it is too late. I sealed the bargain in the long days and nights of childhood.

When I was a child I did not think about morality as it applied to writing, the way I would later be compelled to do. Mostly I made up stories, spun them out of whole cloth — I trusted in my imagination, and in the books I devoured daily, romances and mysteries and science fiction paperbacks I carted home by the armload from the library. Those were the books I wanted to duplicate, to see my name swirled on some cheap paper cover. I would transport readers to distant planets, immerse them in the angst of steamy relationships I had not experienced myself, tickle them into terror with wild grotesqueries. Everything then was about escape. As I descended into the misery of adolescence, it was fiction that promised rescue. I saw the family drama around me and the awkward trauma of high school, but these were things I wrote about rarely, in poetry and essays, and the pain there, clarion on the page, was not something I wanted to see. It was not entertainment.

Somewhere, a shift happened. At fourteen, when I ran away from home, the world heaved and changed. I discovered I wanted to record everything that happened to me, as close to the time of its happening as possible, so that I could wash myself of it. The grit and blood would then be ink on the page. I could not stop myself. I wrote obsessively, recording conversations, scenes, and incidents with the diligence of a reporter. I could not bear for time to lapse between the living and the writing, for in that space there was time for the experiences to sink in, there was time for the consequent pain. Years later I would watch a television report about an eccentric man who recorded virtually every minute of his life — every morsel eaten, every itch scratched, every drop of urine excreted. I wondered if he sought the same thing I did, if his compulsion enabled him to detach so completely from himself that he became two people, one who lived and one who stood next to himself, recording the other's motions with pen and notepad.

I did not think about the people who came in and out of my sight, and who made it onto my pages, as separate from myself and the creative endeavour. They were characters, their words and gestures mine to record and use. I was astonished when I first had to work with an editor to disguise the people in my manuscript, to change names and identifying characteristics. To me, it felt like lying, like a cover-up. What was everyone so afraid of? I was willing to embarrass and expose myself in the service of a story, and it surprised me that other people wouldn't be as willing. Art, after all, was everything. There was a time in my life when the only reason I kept living was because I knew that without being alive, no matter how much I hated it, I could not write. And that was the necessary thing, the one tie to the earth. There was nothing else of comparable value. Not even my family, not the woman who had given birth to me nor the man whom I loved more than anyone in the world and whom I would have given everything to protect. If they did not understand my commitment to my writing, if they stood in its way, then I would have to leave them. I would have to write about them, which meant seeing them as they were, not through a filter of filial love and obligation.

I remember that at age nine my teacher arranged a session for me with the school psychiatrist. The doctor wanted to speak to my mother as well, and when my mother and I walked home afterwards she bent down and told me to never tell anyone about the visit to the psychiatrist. It was a shameful secret, like an intimate disease, nothing the neighbours needed to know. Already, I did not think I could oblige. How could I maintain the facade of a dutiful, high-achieving daughter from a hard-working immigrant family, when so much roiled within me? Yet it was assumed that I would not be tumbled by passions, immobilized by depression, throttled by rage, that I would not break through the skin of the world they had created for me and search in the wilderness for my own self, which sometimes slipped through my fingers like quicksilver. It was assumed that I would never look at my own parents as if I were a stranger, without empathy, instead of seeing them as two figures in a softly focused portrait, the hallowed mother and father, to be obeyed and respected. But what I desired more than anything was to write about what I saw, and I felt that if the words were good enough, if they captured the singular moment, then no one would be offended.

Was this naïveté, selfishness, insensitivity? Perhaps it was above all a matter of values. To put it plainly, without any polite disguise, I valued writing over relationships. How could writing be lonely? Even now, I don't see how it can be. It's when I am not writing that the emptiness opens like a giant flower, and I wander the streets disenfranchised, with no more purpose to my time on earth than a bored housewife who stretches out an hour's worth of chores to fill a day. But the times when I am truly absorbed in my writing have grown further and further apart and, oddly, I do not mourn this. I do wish it were easier, the way it once was, when words flowed from my fingertips for hours and I could imagine nothing sweeter than sitting all day in a room pouring them onto the page. Now they come grudgingly, sporadically, in short bursts followed by lengthy hiatuses during which the blank page stares ruthlessly back at me and I am the first to look away. But perhaps, after all, this is a sign of health, of my entry into the human world.

When I was fifteen and lived in a foster home I shared the house with, among others, the foster parent's niece, who was two years younger than me. A few years ago I saw her again at a party, and we recalled the teenagers we had been. She was living with a man, and not long after would become a mother. She had turned into a grave, mature woman, and it was hard to reconcile all this with the leggy, energetic teen she had been. She looked at me and saw a different person entirely, too. "You were always writing. I kind of thought there was something wrong with you," she said. "There was always this tap, tap, tap, and it was you in the kitchen, on the typewriter." She screwed up her face to imitate the maniacal look I had had on my face as my fingers flew across the keyboard.

I complained that I had quite the opposite problem now — I spent a lot of time and energy doing everything possible to avoid sitting down and writing — and she looked at me solemnly. "Well, maybe you're normal now." The funny thing was that this change didn't trouble me. I sometimes missed the obsessiveness I felt towards writing when I was growing up, but part of it was still there, would always be there, and in the meantime I had developed some sort of self independent of the writing. Once, I would have hated the person I had become; I would have seen myself as a traitor, as someone who had let down my writing god and the fervent child I had been, because I had grown up to do all the things I had vowed I would never do — I had wanted other things, and people, as much as I had wanted to write; I had become distracted by other, sometimes frivolous, desires; I had even contemplated abandoning writing and doing something entirely different with my life. It was all blasphemy, and I would have punished myself feverishly for it as a child, far more than my parents ever could have punished me for not bringing home the straight As that would lead eventually to medical school. I would have made thirty-five New Year's Eve resolutions, as I did one year when I was twelve or thirteen, vowing in all of them to be a better person.

I believed that writing was the answer to everything, that it would never fail to save me. The latter has proved true: when I was able to transform the tangle of an experience into words on the page, that experience felt justified for me, redeemed. It did not matter how ugly it had been, how badly I might have damaged myself or others in the process; there it was, whole and transformed, in black and white. It was my curious sense of what was right and good. But writing has not been the answer to everything. Perhaps this is the realization that I have been grappling with for years, and mourning. Like the death of a beloved, I still cannot believe it. I grew up thinking it would provide every sustenance and that I should not want for anything else as long as I had it.

A few years ago, I spoke with another writer about the work I was creating while in a relationship. I felt that I loved the man I was with, but the poems and stories I was writing might have indicated otherwise. When I lay in this man's arms, I felt close to him, content, and my vision blurred sleepily. I might have been a kitten or a newborn, that uncomplicated. But when I wrote about the relationship there was no kindness or mercy in my observing gaze. I did not quite understand it. Which was the true self? "Anyone reading these pieces would think I never loved him," I lamented to the other writer. "They would think I was cruel. How can I write about him like he's a complete stranger when I feel so much for him?"

"It's in a writer's nature to betray," he replied matter-of-factly.

Was that a facile comment, a glib response to a complex question? It was true that the first time I wrote about somebody I cared for — saw them not through the fuzzy, rose-coloured distortion of affection, but under a glaring light that forgave no flaw — I felt a distinct drop of disappointment. It was the same disappointment I felt the first time my lover came to me in my dreams as, inevitably, my father. There was a sense of defeat; I felt that this must surely not have been love after all, if the writing could be so clear and cruel. I wanted to see only through the eyes of love. I wanted to believe I was capable of that blindness, which was a form of intimacy. Because when the first words tumbled out, the first poem or story I knew I could not show that person, but that I would eventually feel compelled to publish — thereby dooming the relationship — I knew it was over. I had pushed him away, and now there was a distance between us, a secret as divisive as an adulterous affair. But that was the writing's way of saving me, too. I knew then that I was detached from this person, that he could not consume me, that I was not so vulnerable before him that his least abandonment could destroy me. I was safe in a tower behind the high wall of words.

For a long time the writing was all that existed. I could not even justify going out with friends and enjoying myself if I did not come home with a scrap of conversation, an image, a line to be plowed into the prose. That time of pleasure would feel like time wasted. I was always watching, and soon had to confront the question of whether it was possible to be a participant in one's own life if one was also the observer. I envied people who seemed able to let themselves go, who had an appetite for experience and emotion, who could live inside the moment and inhabit it with their whole, un-selfconscious selves. The only time I seemed able to do that was when I was so drunk or stoned that the world was obliterated, so that became a kind of holiday from watching, which was a form of unceasing work.

Even now it is almost impossible for me to see my work from the point of view of one of my subjects. It is alarming to run into someone whom I have written about, see the white shock of their faces in the grocery store or the movie theatre. Like children, we look quickly away and pretend we haven't seen each other. In an odd way they are no longer real people to me, and I am surprised to discover that they still exist in the world and not just between the covers of a book, where I have confined them.

So, something is lost each time. It hardly seems worth it, upon reflection. But at the time it is — this is the only choice, the only road, there is no other. To not publish something for fear of losing someone's affections — that still seems to me to be the ultimate cowardice, the unforgivable weakness. That would be the moment I turn my back on the child I was, all the promises I made to myself there in the darkness. That would be the moment I step in front of the speeding truck and its force bears down on me with all the weight of the mortal world.

To some degree, that decision has been taken out of my hands, thanks to the laws regarding defamation and privacy. This was something I never thought I would have to consider, these outwardly imposed strictures on one's writing. I struggle to understand the rationale behind them, and how they reflect the morals and values of our time. I try to grasp the importance of a person's sense of self, individuals' right to present themselves as they wish to others — which already indicates to me the presence of false selves, images they are projecting to hide the true selves beneath — but it is elusive to me. I can never empathize with the subject for longer than I can entertain the idea of eternity. It slips away, and when I hurry through the maze to try to find it again, I cannot. I cannot contain it in myself, because the truth is that I expect others to consider themselves and their interests secondary to the greater cause of the writing, as I have done myself. Much of what I have written causes me embarrassment and humiliation; much of what I write and publish I cannot bear to read afterwards, because it is so revealing I can hardly stand its existence in the world; but for me to put the interests of my own privacy first, ahead of the work, continues to be untenable.

I suppose I don't understand the notion of privacy very well. There has always been this strange urgent need in me to make the private public, to turn things inside out so that what typically lives hidden in darkness is exposed to the light. I wanted everyone to live that way. I harboured contempt for those who kept key aspects of their lives hidden. It reminded me too much of the men who circled the blocks in their cars when I was a teenager, those men with their wives and children and houses in the suburbs.

Still, I keep trying to understand it from the perspective of the other. What if I told someone that I might write about him — that I might describe his every flaw, convey a personal comment he made to me one night over a drink, write about how he looked the last time he picked his nose? Should those involved with a writer, especially romantically, expect to see themselves in that person's work? I've seen it over and over, among the writers I know — their affairs, their relationships, their marriages are plowed back into their work, perhaps not apparent to the casual reader, but almost embarrassingly transparent to those who know them.

But even among writers there is dissent about this idea of using the lives of those around you in your work. A young writer told me recently about attending a lecture by a leading Canadian author who told her audience that she did not use people from her life in her work, and thought that those writers who did so were irresponsible. This young writer, who was working on some beautifully crafted short stories based on painful family experiences, felt even more conflict than she had already been feeling about possibly hurting her family after the lecture. "When she said that, I felt a chill in my heart," she told me, her struggle plain in her voice. I encouraged her to continue working on her stories, and countered the lecturer's opinion with my own passionate opinions on the subject. But it later occurred to me that maybe it is all about worth. What is most important to the writer — their relationships or their writing? After all, one seems to thrive at the expense of the other.

Once in a while, the sadness of that catches up with me, surprising me. I was giving a reading to a large roomful of people, hundreds whose faces I couldn't see in the darkness beyond the lit stage. In that swatch of light, reading part of a short story that was based on a relationship that had ended, I suddenly felt a regret that caught me off guard. Had I exploited my relationship with that man, used him to provide moments that could be replicated on the page? Might the relationship have survived had I not scrutinized it so closely? I felt as if I knew nothing about what it meant to be human, to live or feel without watching. I began to detach from the sadness and examine it like an unusual pebble that had washed up on the shore, as I continued reading. I felt the pain of the lost relationship — all that remained of it was these words on a page, which were without delusion, possibly cruel, certainly exposing — but at the same time I became a voyeur to the pain, observing it as I had observed the relationship. It seemed after all that I had something in common with the middle-aged or older men who would say to me, after a lifetime of relationships, "You know, I don't think I know what love is. I don't think I've ever been in love." When they said these things, I always felt then as if I had swallowed a stone, which sat in my stomach, hard and cold. So this was what there was, after a lifetime: you realize you don't know anything about love, that you've never been in love. But this inability to feel, this dry, empty space, was perhaps one I inhabited as well.

It is a strangely journalistic approach to literature, this fierce desire to record rather than to create. This satisfaction at finding the phrases that describe people and events as they are, and not always asking, "What if?"

Why is it that imagination is valued over recorded experience? A writer friend of mine says that he finds it impossible to take seriously his friends' novels and other works of fiction, no matter how well-written they may be, because he can see through the thin layers of disguise straight to the autobiographical source. Recently I attended a reading at which the authors stood on the stage and answered questions from the audience. Somehow the topic turned to "pure" fiction rather than fiction that came from lived experience, which the authors repeatedly disdained. I was a great admirer of one of these writers, portions of whose work seemed largely autobiographical, and now I had to think that either he was being disingenuous or I was wrong, that his close scrutiny of relationships was spun entirely out of the ether and not from anything he had experienced.

Perhaps one of the reasons writers are so vehement about not identifying their work as autobiographical is because, of course, it never is simply that. The most nakedly autobiographical work of fiction still has elements of the created, still wanders off into "what if?" territory. In some readers' eyes, an admission that something is autobiographical — and the very word *admission* implies some sort of guilt — would mean that every line sprang unadulterated from the author's lived experience, which would be an incorrect assumption.

I have an acquaintance, a psychiatrist, who when she was growing up felt towards medicine the way I did towards writing. She knew from the time she was five that she wanted to be a doctor, and pursued it with single-minded passion and focus, attending medical school with full scholarships. No one, meeting her at a party or on the dance floor, would guess that this young, attractive woman with the blue nail polish and tinkly laughter is a psychiatrist. Indeed, she doesn't like to announce what she does for a living, doesn't enjoy watching another's attitude towards her visibly shift and change — she prefers to socialize with people who aren't doctors, and avoids the romantic advances of men in the medical profession. Like mine, her entire life has been pointed in one direction, and now she is beginning to wonder what else is out there. One evening at a dinner party we started talking about our work and how we were thinking of changing careers, of veering off one path and onto another, and we became impassioned, because we discovered that our feelings were the same. There was the same sense of guilt at even contemplating change, a sense of loyalty to the past, to the dedicated children we were. There was the same desire to leave before we came to hate and resent our work; already we could hear ourselves whine and complain about what we did for a living, and we didn't like that, didn't want to wait until everything had been spoiled for us before we went elsewhere. There was the same eagerness and curiosity about what else might exist for us in the world, coupled with the same fear we had as people who had only ever known one thing.

We spoke in loud whispers, as if what we were saying was a kind of heresy. I remembered a journalist asking me what my greatest disappointment had been, and to her surprise, and mine, I immediately had said, "My writing." But it is true. All my life I thought writing would be the answer to everything. I thought it was the key that would open every door; I thought it would provide for me everything I could ever imagine needing or wanting. I thought if I were a published writer I would finally be perfect. I sought perfection so furiously as a child, but every day would be ruined within the first few hours as soon as I committed what I construed to be an imperfect thought, word, or gesture. The rest of the day would be destroyed, a shambles; I could only hope for a perfect tomorrow. I thought that being a writer would somehow end all of that. But it never happened.

A woman I know who used to write poetry says she's glad she has stopped. "I don't know how I would have coped if I'd kept going. It took me to a very difficult place. I think eventually it would have destroyed me."

Who would choose to be destroyed? I remember a visit to the family doctor, a middle-aged Chinese woman, when I was eleven or twelve. Accompanying me to the reception area afterwards, where my family was waiting, she asked cheerfully, "So, what would you like to be when you grow up?"

"A writer."

"How about a doctor, hmm, like me? Wouldn't you like that? You could come and talk to me about being a doctor, and I'll show you what I do."

"No. I'm going to be a writer," I said firmly, swelling with the certainty of it.

I could see my father's smile vanishing, the furrows emerging between his eyebrows. My parents' embarrassed laughter, their profuse thank yous as we left the building. They were furious on the ride home; I remember my father's tight, bitter voice, burning the air, how the afternoon crumpled like a paper flower thrown into the flames. How dare I be so disrespectful? My writing, my writing — all I could talk about was my writing. The doctor was being so kind, encouraging me to join her esteemed profession; I should listen to her, I should be grateful for her attention, I should aspire to be like her. I sat in the back seat, saying nothing. I could have just kept quiet, nodded politely in the doctor's office, and the afternoon would have been saved. My parents would have beamed at me in the reception room, proud of their healthy daughter, body and mind intact, who would one day grow up to wear a white coat and a stethoscope slung around her neck. Who would choose to ruin their hopeful vision? They had come such a long way, sacrificed so much, to see it fulfilled. But my writing was like an actual physical entity, to which I had to be loyal. I had to defend it and fight for it and protect it, always. I looked out the window while my father's disappointment, edged with panic — he was perhaps realizing that this might not be a phase after all, that it was possible I intended to do what I said and there was nothing he could do to stop it — flooded through the interior of the car.

A reviewer once wrote that she had the feeling I could see through people's clothes. I cherished that compliment, because as a writer I have always wanted to see through surfaces. I have a soft spot for the houses and towns replicated in miniature in some museums, down to the tiny roll of toilet paper in the bathroom, the cigarette pack not much bigger than a fingernail paring that lies on the coffee table. I can spend hours moving from scene to scene, looking inside houses with one wall torn away to expose the drama within — the miniature father embracing the maid in the children's nursery, the naked wife huddled in a puddle of watery glue in the bathtub, her small violin-shaped back turned to the prurient eye. Eagerly I try to absorb the details behind every window before moving on to the next created diorama, always with the tugging sensation that I have missed something, neglected to peek into an interesting corner, that indeed a whole corner store or chapel in a town has escaped my notice. What exquisite little treasures had I missed — a row of tinned tomatoes with their speck-sized labels peeling off, the Biblical scene in a radiant stained glass window that I could balance on the tip of my finger? Looking at these models seems like what I do as a writer, what I love — examining these private lives, charmingly self-involved, going about their daily business, exposed to the observing eye reflected like a giant's in the glass skin that protects their world. I always feel as if I could stay there for days, breathing in the musty air of the museum, peering in one window after another, down the cleavage of the corseted barmaid inside the tavern in the 1800s town where the men leer drunkenly over tiny plastic mugs of beer capped with plastic foam, into the bassinet over which the nanny bends, her painted face tilting a genuinely sweet smile, while in the library of the grand house the master wearing wire-framed spectacles reads his leather-bound book and his wife sits at a distance from him, her knitting in her lap, looking frustrated.

At some point, perhaps, I will no longer be content with looking. I will want to shrink to the size of someone who could sleep comfortably in a bed the length of a matchbox and cross over to this other world, perhaps when the exhibits are resting — when night has fallen over the towns and the cities, and tiny twinkles of light sparkle from bedroom windows behind drawn curtains, and flames glow red in the fireplaces, and everyone is safe and secure inside their log cabins, three-bedroom houses, and New York penthouse apartments. The mustachioed proprietor can no longer be seen behind his counter at the canned goods store; the pulpit and pews of the church are empty. All the fashionable ladies have left the stores with their hats and parasols, and have gone home to their houses where a light is always left on in the downstairs hall though the rooms are swathed in mysterious darkness. I will find some small corner for myself, and when the electric day breaks over the world I will be one of the people living inside one of those houses, going about my day with a list of errands as long as my arm, unaware of anything larger beyond the painted blue sky.

Perhaps I will be brave and choose instead to enter the exhibit of the future, the one with the barbell-shaped spaceship pocked with hundreds of tiny port-holes that revolves in the starry sky, above the cold surface of the planet. I will be one of the figures in the elevator that runs up and down the exterior of the highrise in the centre of the alien city. I will wear pink thigh-high boots and futuristic materials that crackle and give off a dull sheen. I will believe that this is real because I will have never known anything else and cannot imagine that there is another world, only a partition away, where cows graze in meadows, trains trundle through tunnels cut into the green mountains, and miners, their little hands and faces coarsely blackened, haul buckets of coal on pulleys up to the surface.

Whichever world I choose, it will be the whole world to me. I will inhabit it fully, engaging myself in every detail, finally a participant instead of an observer.

ANATOMY OF A
LIBEL LAWSUIT

"CAN YOU GET SUED for winking?" a books columnist asked me recently. We were talking about writers who use real people in their work, and he mentioned attending a reading at which the author was asked if the characters in his book were based on a family who was known to be litigious. He said no, and the columnist's heart sank. "It was so clear his book was about them! I felt less respect for him at that moment."

"But what could he have said? They could have sued him if he had admitted it was them."

"I don't know." He looked out the window, then gave me a small smile. "Maybe he should have said no, but winked at the audience as he did so. Surely you can't get sued for winking."

This is a story that begins with a stranger at the door, bearing a message. It was a winter afternoon in 1997, ten days before Christmas. He said my name questioningly and I said yes, that was who I was. It was only later it would seem to me that the courier's lips twitched with a knowing smirk as he passed a flat manila envelope into my hands and turned away.

I carried the envelope to the couch and opened it, and a few crisp sheets slid out. The moment when the letterhead registered, stern black letters on the cream page, I experienced a sinking sensation. A few months earlier I had published a memoir in *Vancouver* magazine about my relationship with another writer, W.P. (Bill) Kinsella, entitled "Me & W.P." We had become romantically involved when I was twenty-four and he was sixty; in writing about the experience, I had been trying to make sense of our two-year involvement and why it had, almost inevitably, failed. The responses to my article had been mixed; some readers identified with the story and found it insightful, while others felt I had behaved abominably by writing about an intimate relationship. Now Kinsella's lawyer was threatening legal action against the magazine's publisher, its editors, and me.

I sensed a shift then, as if I already recognized this to be the beginning of a process that until now had been mysterious to me. The power of language started to take on a whole new meaning — in the eyes of the law, where an author's intentions were considered irrelevant, words were examined as carefully as jewels under a microscope. That day, looking down at the pages on my lap, I felt poised at the beginning of something. As my eyes dashed down the draft of the unfiled statement of claim, with its accusing points set out in the severe-sounding language of the law, I was already learning something new. The word *plaintiff*, for example: I had never known it referred to the person launching a lawsuit. It sounded a little like *sheriff* or *bailiff*, so I'd always assumed it described some policeman-like person who stood in the courtroom wearing a uniform, his meaty arms crossed over his chest.

But no, the plaintiff was someone who had once woken next to me in a spill of sunlight. My pulse pounded. His name as plaintiff suddenly looked like the name of a stranger, someone whose actions I could not predict any more than I could predict those of a person passing me on the street. Even without the personal aspect of the situation, it was unsettling to think that anything I had written could be untrue, or could provoke such a litany of harms done and damages deserved. Defamation and invasion of privacy. What did those terms really mean? A tiny burst of fear ignited inside me like a sparkler, shivering and crackling.

Much later, when I asked a criminal lawyer what a law school education could offer, he said simply, "It provides a structure upon which the world fits." On that day, no structure was evident to me — I could not see the world's skeleton, its cage of ribs, its spine. I had no context in which to place the contents of the manila envelope. The arrival of the letter was almost like an initiation, as if a veil were lifting from something that had previously been hidden. Soon I would realize that most of the stories on the news involved the law in some way, and that I was at the beginning of a path that was familiar to many people.

Two days later, the editor of *Vancouver* magazine and I met with a lawyer. He worked at one of the large firms downtown, with its cavernous views of water, mountains, and evergreens. He greeted us in the waiting area, giving me a long, measuring look as we shook hands, and led us back to his office, which overlooked the water. Christmas cards from the media outlets he defended against libel actions were clustered brightly by the window. There was a framed photograph of a child angled on his desk; in other circumstances it would have been polite to inquire about her, or to make some passing remark about the weather, but here the clock was ticking.

The lawyer was in his mid-thirties, and had an earnest, likeable manner. Behind his glasses his eyes were almond-shaped and tilted upwards, and he kept them fixed on us as we answered his questions and his handwriting flowed illegibly across a lined pad. I tried to describe the plaintiff, the tangled intentions or single burning motivation that might be behind his behaviour, and felt helpless. It was as if I was talking about someone I had never met. I thought about how mysterious our next actions are, even to ourselves, let alone to others, and the forces that lay behind them — the scrap of childhood memory, the bitterly nursed resentment, the tapped well of hidden rage. I felt my face growing hot as the hour passed. The persistent feeling of dread sometimes flared into frustration, because what I longed to express was my obsessive need to write without censor. When I was a child my writing was the one thing I refused to have controlled or taken away; I guarded fiercely what I thought was my right to write about anything I chose. I prized it above every human relationship, sensing even then that the deceptions and silences often required to maintain relationships with others would be shattered in the process of writing about them.

"Don't worry, we won't sell you down the river," the editor said suddenly, sensing the worry that clouded my thoughts. It turned out that the handwritten document Bill and I had signed during our relationship (it read, in its entirety, "W.P. Kinsella and Evelyn Lau agree that we will never take legal action against each other on anything we may write or publish.") wasn't legally binding, though it would be helpful in our defence. When the meeting ended, the lawyer told us it was now his job to worry about the case, not ours, and we walked out into the blue winter day. What was it that squeezed my heart, made it trip too fast? We decided to drop in at a media reception in a hotel down the street; a few journalists we knew were there, and when they asked how things were going, what was new, I hated the lie in my voice, which was simply an omission, an absence — things were going fine, nothing was new. It was better not to tell anyone about the lawyer's letter until an actual statement of claim had been filed, since we were still hoping we could dissuade Bill from pursuing the lawsuit. But I felt that by not saying anything, I was lying. I always said everything; there was a kind of safety in dispensing something personal out in the world, scattering its seeds among many, in the light of day. Instead, this was taking on the quality of a secret, a hard and bitter seed, buried in some dark place inside me.

The lawsuit raised not only legal but moral issues, which I sought to understand. I read everything I could find about the law of defamation; consequently, I began spotting potential libels everywhere, and it seemed that everyone around me was always slandering others in the course of casual conversation. Even while reading an excerpt of a literary bestseller, John Bayley's *Elegy for Iris*, a line from the draft statement of claim kept floating above the page: "disparaging, demeaning, humiliating and embarrassing references . . . to their mode of dress, taste and physical appearance." Bayley's descriptions of his wife, her lack of taste in clothes and her lack of beauty, were exactly the sort of clear-sighted observations for which a writer strives. He did not see her through a filter of sentiment or empty praise, and that was what made his portrait of her so strong. But if an unflinching description could be deemed worthy of a lawsuit, would writers have to think twice before describing someone in anything other than a flattering light?

I began to compile a list of books by writers that chronicled, in intimate detail, their relationships with other writers. The ways in which their subjects responded to finding themselves in the role of muse were varied, but did not involve the courts. When Simone de Beauvoir wrote, first in thinly disguised fiction and then in detailed memoir, about her affair with Nelson Algren, he responded by trashing her books in a review for *Harper's*. He never forgave her for publishing long excerpts from his love letters to her; when he was in his seventies he shouted during an interview, enraged, "Love letters should be private . . . But this woman flung the door open and called in the public and the press." The reporter left in a hurry, worried about the author's health; the next day, Algren was found dead of a heart attack.

Sometimes the subject of the memoir responded with his own version of the relationship, as Philip Roth did with *I Married a Communist* after his ex-wife Claire Bloom published her account of their miserable marriage in *Leaving a Doll's House*. Or occasionally someone else leapt to the subject's defence — when George Sand wrote about her affair with a younger man in *Elle et Lui*, his brother published a more sympathetic account of the relationship a year later, cleverly calling it *Lui et Elle*.

I found it illuminating that these confessional writers tended to be vilified by critics and the public, as if they were committing a literary version of leaping up with fists flying on *The Jerry Springer Show*. Even the elderly, esteemed writer Lillian Ross, who wrote about her forty-year affair with the deceased New Yorker editor William Shawn in *Here but Not Here*, was taken to task in reviews for causing unnecessary grief to his still-living widow. *Sir Vidia's Shadow*, Paul Theroux's account of his former friendship with V.S. Naipaul, while lacking the possible sexual titillation factor of the others memoirs, nonetheless provoked similarly hot-headed cries of betrayal; Joyce Maynard's *At Home in the World*, which revealed details of her relationship with the famously private J.D. Salinger, including revelations about his bulimia and their neurotic sex life, created a wave of public moral affront.

I wondered if readers were not taking these works too

personally. Perhaps they imagined themselves in books written by their own lovers, forgetting that neither they nor their partners were writers, and that there was a long if not always honourable tradition of writers writing about their relationships with each other. It happens more frequently than most people are aware; one day, browsing through an obscure literary magazine called *Gargoyle*, I came across an essay by Amy Halloran, who wrote provocatively about sleeping with the author and playwright Spalding Gray in hopes of warranting a mention in his next work, and thereby furthering her own career. And when I tried to compile a list of writers who have in their work used the first or last names of real people for characters based on those people, the sheer volume of examples forced me to give up.

I wished it was impossible to take successful legal action against a work that has literary merit, but realized that was perhaps an unrealistic vision of how the world should work. Yet some friends told me that while they did not mind literary kiss-and-tell memoirs because they were well written, they did object to, say, Liona Boyd's account of her eight-year affair with Pierre Trudeau in *In Her Own Key*, because they did not consider her autobiography to be a work of literature.

Nearly all the memoirs I came across were written by women. This reminded me of Doris Lessing's observation, which I supposed could also be construed as a warning, in her autobiography *Walking in the Shade*: "A woman writer, putting love before literature, when love lets her down will then make literature out of love."

It was January 1998. After the holidays we produced papers — letters, press clippings — supporting the facts and opinions in my memoir. The editor tried to comfort and reassure me: "There's no need for you to worry. If worse come to worst, the company will pick up the tab." But somehow it was about more than that. The statement of claim hadn't yet been filed, but a pea-soup fog of depression had descended around me. In the mornings, when I tried to approach my desk, a dark wave washed over me and I ended up sitting on the sofa, gazing out the window, sunk in the conviction that there was no point in writing anything new because it would only lead to other lawsuits. Much of my work, after all, was personal, revelatory, and based on actual events. On a deeper level, one that I could not yet articulate to myself, there was also the certainty that anything else I wrote would lead to losing other people in my life, as it had in the past.

My psychiatrist observed that the feelings orbiting inside me — pain, anxiety, anger — were the ones that should have occurred at the end of the relationship with Bill, the ones I prevented myself from experiencing by writing the article. And, of course, those feelings originated in my childhood, and truly belonged there; I should have gone through them the first time around.

Instead, like the person who keeps getting reincarnated in order to face again and again the moment where the needle is stuck on the record, so do I, in one relationship after the next, act out on a tiny stage the larger drama of child and parents. Whenever any emotion threatens to become unmanageable, I always detach, look upon the people involved as characters and the situation as a story, and turn on the cool gaze of the observer rather than the desperate one of a participant. In retrospect it seems powerfully useless, to expend so much energy protecting yourself from emotions that, suppressed, create a grey broth of depression, leading to therapy in which you have to painfully experience all those feelings you've blocked in the first place. It doesn't make sense but it is what I do, rationalizing that perhaps this time two plus two won't equal four in this emotional arithmetic.

At the beginning of March, Bill's statement of claim was filed in B.C. Supreme Court. The next morning was grey and rainy and the day smelled new. Sometime in the next few weeks the trees would don the faintest, palest green shroud, the hint of leaves about to bloom. I went to the library and found a copy of *Canadian Author & Bookman*, in which a short story Bill had written about our relationship had been published. I read it and looked out the windows down onto the brick concourse. Where did all that feeling go? The love that was in the story — how had it led to this? It was there, the feelings he had surely once had, captured on the page, in black and white, just as if they were permanent. As if somewhere in a parallel existence, in the world of stories, we were still lying together on a bed in a hotel room in Bermuda. It seemed strange that the story could capture a time, so fleeting, forever on the page, but that in the rest of the floating world it could be gone. Where did feelings go when they disappeared? Did they leave a chemical trace somewhere in our minds, so that if we could look inside ourselves we would see via the patterns of neurons some of the important things that had happened to us in our lifetimes? If so, how was I being shaped by the lawsuit? What was I learning?

That evening the brief hopefulness, the smell of morning, evaporated. I paced the floor of my apartment. When yet another reporter called, the anxiety I felt squeezed my thoughts, and the white fog of blankness descended again. The nothing, the depression. I curled up on the sofa, sick with the welling nausea and clamping pain of a migraine, covering my eyes from the faint light from the window.

A writer friend called, shaking his head over the lawsuit. "I thought the way you dealt with the end of the relationship was perverse, but his way of dealing with it is even more perverse!" He queried me about the lawsuit with a kind of ravenous curiosity that cheered me up, because it reminded me of my own detachment and how everything can be, objectively, interesting if you're a writer.

"What does the writ actually look like?" he asked eagerly. "I mean, is it splendid, does it have seals on it and so on? Can you frame it and hang it on the wall in the centre of your room as an *objet d'art*? I rather thought it might come with, you know, tassels or something . . ."

When I told him I'd only received a faxed copy of the statement of claim from our lawyer, he sounded so disappointed that we both started to laugh.

By mid-March I was feeling disillusioned about the reactions many of my friends and acquaintances were having towards my memoir and the lawsuit. Some of them felt that the lawsuit was deserved retribution for a moral wrong I had committed; others unabashedly said that they envied the publicity the litigation was bringing. At a party, an acquaintance pushed her face close to mine and said, "If you'd written about me that way, I'd have sued you, too!" She wasn't the first person to say this, and though I laughed awkwardly, I was hurt. The lawsuit had been widely reported in the media, and my ego had suffered a few blows from criticisms voiced about my article, which was taking on the larger life Bill had given it by suing. The editor was receiving requests from media and curious people for copies of the article. Journalists were discussing it on television, on the radio, writing columns about it. People who had not been aware of its existence prior to the lawsuit were now reading it for the first time and expressing their opinions.

People kept asking me why I wrote the piece, and I hardly knew what to say; this question particularly confounded me when it came from other writers, who I thought would have understood. It was as if they were asking that same question about a poem of mine, or a story, or a book. Why did a writer write anything? It was what was burning inside them at the time, it was the story they had to tell before they could go on to tell other stories. But now the prospect of writing was repulsive to me. I kept thinking that anything I might write would lead to other losses; the effect was feelings of defeat and inertia. What was it about writing that once made me feel chosen, immortal, inviolable? As a child I believed that as long as I was working on something, nothing could injure me — I could step in front of a two-ton truck and remain unscathed, because the writing was so necessary that as long as I was doing it, I couldn't be harmed. There was a sense of the words being larger than anything, including myself. F. Scott Fitzgerald, after a writing binge, wrote, ". . . in every story, it was the extra I had. Now it has gone and I am just like you now." The writing was the extra in me, and who was I without it?

By the end of March we had filed our statement of defence, which looked strong and gave me hope. The magazine editor and I had lunch one day with another editor who told us that he had been served legal letters or sued a total of four times in connection with various publications. The first time he was only twenty-two, and he grimaced at the memory. "I had a few sweaty-panted weeks there, believe me."

In mid-May, during intermission at the opening of a musical, I glimpsed Bill's face ahead of me just as a girl-friend and I were about to walk past him. He had changed his appearance, cutting off his dyed hair and growing a beard, and it was easy to think that this was not the person I had known. Nevertheless, the second act passed by me in a blur of noise and light that made no sense. After the musical there was a reception at a nearby hotel where, to the amusement of some onlook-ers, Bill and his girlfriend and I circled the room all evening trying not to bump into each other. Once, he turned to head in my direction, saw me, and made a sharp right, motioning his girlfriend to follow. Our eyes had met dead on, and I could not interpret his look. It amazed me that someone I had observed so closely could now be mysterious to me, unreadable.

The depression was a black sea spilling in along the edges of the day, rising above the barricades and overflowing. Sometimes I woke from dreams in which I was back with Bill — in those rare but lit moments in the relationship when things were good — and I felt stricken. The darkness would surely lift if I could only talk to him. The urge was so great, a heated pressure building in me, that if we weren't engaged in litigation, I would have called him.

My day's work was getting out of bed, which took hours. I craved sleep like it was a lover. The normal machinations of the day, the small tasks of standing under the shower stream, of loading the dishwasher, defeated me. There was a kind of recoiling horror at the thought of brushing my teeth, picking clothes off the floor. Even the fact that I had just finished writing another book provided no pleasure, only another ominous storm cloud on the horizon. John Cheever, in his last diary entry, when he was sick, wrote, "Now I am undressing to go to bed, and my fatigue is so overwhelming that I am undressing with the haste of a lover." I knew what that felt like, and yet I wasn't sick, wasn't old and dying. All day long I dreamt of the earliest time when I could disappear again into sleep, into that white negation. This was the closest I could come to stopping — this long pause, this death in life, the hours of drinking when I did go out, then throwing up and sleep.

In early June "Me & W.P." won in the Human Experience category at the Western Magazine Awards. At the foot of the stairs, as I arrived, a journalist who was also up for an award told me urgently that he thought my writing the article was morally wrong. Together we climbed the stairs and he kept glancing at me, perhaps kindly, to show that he meant no harm. Still, I felt like a chastised child, made inarticulate by the desire to defend myself. I felt strangled with anger — because of course I only wanted to be liked, approved of, like everyone else. Why did the writing make that impossible? Afterwards, as we celebrated in the bar with a group of people, the editor and his wife seemed very close. They were like two teenagers, their fingers entwined, his leg over the arm of her chair, and I felt a clutch of sadness watching them.

It seemed I had never understood the idea of the right to privacy, never empathized with it or thought about it until now. From the beginning I had had this urge to present people as I saw them, to describe the faces beneath the masks as nakedly and unsentimentally as possible. I wanted to peel back the disguising layers, the gloss, to expose the true selves underneath. I had always been interested in exploring people who presented one face to the world and another in their private lives. If anything, this formed the basis of all my writing — all my work, from my first book onwards, had had this as a theme. As a writer I was both fascinated and repelled by that division, the tension between those two selves. On some level I deplored people who maintained this duplicity; it reminded me too much of the men who came down to the streets to buy sex from girls the age of their daughters. Why would anyone do anything in private that they considered to be so shameful or wrong that they would litigate if it were made public? A therapist I knew once told me that he wouldn't mind if any of the details of his private life were made public because, as he said simply, "I don't do things I'd be ashamed of if other people knew about them."

Over the years I had heard and read enough author interviews to become well versed in all the ways in which a writer could deny that a work was based on their own lives or on those of people they knew. On occasion these vigorous, sometimes offended denials rang false to my ears. These writers risked sounding coy and disingenuous at best, outright dishonest at worst. In interviews to promote my own books I was frequently grilled about autobiographical influences, and I heard the same evasive words tripping from my own tongue, the empty answer that gave nothing away. The true answer was often complex — the strands of memory, imagination, fact, fantasy, creation, and catharsis were inextricably woven together — but I sometimes longed for the brave soul who would say simply, "Yes, of course. This character is based on so-and-so. I've changed a few details, and made some stuff up, but otherwise it's that person." But, as a lawyer who defended many defamation and privacy cases said to me, "That'd be great! But the law doesn't allow you to do that without putting yourself at risk."

The decision to write about people in one's life, and risk losing their affection or raising their ire, is hardly a simple one for most writers. Graham Greene once said that every genuine writer has a sliver of ice lodged in his heart. When I was approached by people who were angst-ridden about portraying their loved ones in poetry or prose, I told them that the work should be their most important consideration, that the power of the writing should be paramount. That they should never dilute their writing with the thin milk of fear over how someone might react. I perceived it as a weakness when they worried about the tearful accusations, the doors slammed on their relationships. I thought that if they were truly serious about their writing, only the work would matter. Yet trying to explain this position to others was like speaking an alien language. I was left to wonder if there was something wrong with me, though the question of whether the work or life should come first was one that many writers and artists had grappled with over the centuries.

As the lawsuit progressed, I attempted to understand the situation from the plaintiff's perspective. In a *New*

Yorker article criticizing the erosion of privacy, Jeffrey Rosen argued that "a sexual memoir is the equivalent of a literary strip search, depriving the unsuspecting partner of the most basic attribute of self-definition, which is the ability to control the face we present to the world." But in the precarious balance that is always being struck between one individual's right to privacy and another's right to freedom of expression, I found myself again and again favouring the latter. Lately, lawyers had predicted that the next decade would see a surge in the number of privacy claims filed. What impact would this have on writers? How many works of literature and biography published to date would not have been published if their subjects could have sued successfully because the author had publicly disclosed private facts, or breached some perceived confidence?

Fortunately, there were people who were quite thrilled to find themselves, however exposed or unflatteringly portrayed, in a work of literature. It could be intoxicating, to know that you once said something, gave a look or gesture, memorable enough to be committed to the page. That of all the faces in the crowd, yours was chosen — even if, in print, it turned out not to be the face you thought you were presenting to the world.

By mid-June we were in the documents phase, working with a different lawyer, the one *Vancouver* magazine usually engaged in these situations. For months I had been worrying about the hundreds of notes and letters I had written to Bill during the course of our relationship, keeping no copies because I wanted to give them as though they were gifts, un-selfconscious, unguarded. How sentimental were the letters, how incriminating? Bill had diligently kept copies of every note he had sent me, once even asking me to make a fax copy for him of a letter he'd sent that he had forgotten to duplicate. Now I wished that I had documented everything, written every letter with the understanding that one day it might be read aloud in court.

Whenever my fax machine rang, and papers printed with the law firms' letterheads spiralled out, my body reacted with a spasm of anxiety. The language of the documents was threatening and aggressive, designed to intimidate. If you didn't know better, you would think you were about to lose everything. Adam Gopnik, in a *New Yorker* article about Oscar Wilde, wrote simply, "The law has a certain horrible momentum of its own, and anyone who comes in contact with it can be destroyed."

I spent hours sifting through documents to give to our lawyer. Letters from Bill, poems, the unpublished novel I had written about our relationship, newspaper articles in which either of us talked about the other or that contained information already made public about him that he was now alleging to be private. It was a gruesome task, especially rereading Bill's letters, no longer eagerly, through the eyes of love, but coldly, scrutinizing them for phrases and comments that might prove useful to our case. The letters seemed curious and sad, artifacts from another life. How things changed, after all, feelings too, which I used to think endured and could be relied upon, like furniture. But it was tolerable. It had been nearly a year since the relationship ended, and I no longer had to fight against the sadness or disavow it.

An acquaintance and I had a conversation about writers and their love letters; he said to beware, because while they're writing these letters they could get carried away, drunk on the language. I knew what he meant. One eye was always turned towards posterity glinting on the horizon, so there was something perhaps a bit false about writers' letters. On some level a writer's letter was never only an intimate correspondence between two people but one that potentially enclosed a wide, faceless future reading audience. Max Frisch once wrote, "The writer is afraid of feelings that are not suited to publication . . . all he perceives is considered from the point of view of whether it is worth describing, and he dislikes experiences that can never be expressed in words."

It was around this time, in June, that the litigation began to interest me as a writer. I experienced the first blush of fascination, of being seized by curiosity. I could feel myself detaching, watching, gnawed by a kind of hunger, flush with it as with fever. I had never been interested in the law, had never watched legal dramas on television or read legal thrillers. Now I wanted to write about the law, this country to which I had been temporarily deported. Who were its inhabitants? What was the system they lived under? Gail Anderson-Dargatz, interviewed on CBC-TV's *Bookmark*, talked about her husband undergoing brain surgery, and how while this traumatic event was happening she nonetheless found herself taking mental notes, knowing she would use the experience in her next book. "I think writers are a lot like lawyers," she said, smiling. "We feed off the misfortunes of people, even ourselves."

I began to gravitate towards my friends and acquaintances who were lawyers. I noticed how at parties if people were asked what they did for a living and they were lawyers, they said so with an apologetic grimace, mumbling it out of the corners of their mouths, ducking their heads. Curtains of misery descended over their faces when they were asked about their work, lifted when the subject changed. At dinner parties, where they arrived tired and late, eyes half-lidded, leather cases in hand, straight from the office, they wanted only drinks and conversation about anything but their lives in law. Yet they possessed a knowledge that had become desirable to me; I wanted to understand how their world was structured. It seemed like everywhere I looked now there was the law, manifest. It formed a network beneath the living world; it was a kind of structure that held everything together and aloft. I wanted to familiarize myself with its workings so that it no longer had the power to intimidate me. The law was something I had never thought about before, and now it seemed so integral, the motivation or the restraint behind many of our actions. I wanted to read everything about the tort of defamation, to understand why something I had written could lead to a lawsuit. Why did there need to be laws restricting freedom of expression? What power did the written word possess to inflict injury, and why should the courts intercede? How could someone demand solace and compensation, measured out in dollars, for that injury, as if that perceived blow to reputation or sense of self was as real, as painful and visible, as a limb torn from his body?

I realized that one of the reasons the lawsuit upset me so much was that the restrictions it placed on my freedom of expression reminded me of how I felt as a child living with my parents. A criminal lawyer later explained to me that the driving force of his life had been rage, a bottomless well of it, and that discovering the law in his early twenties had been his life's miracle, because it provided a venue in which he could channel and use his rage. He found he could finally control it by turning it to his advantage in the courtroom. Conversely, my involvement with the law had called up the buried anger in me, the anger of a child. I remembered, as a young teenager, sitting at the piano and my father spitting out, "Your writing, your writing. It's always your writing!" We were having some argument again over my obsession with writing, and this time I dared to talk back.

"You can say anything else, but you can't criticize my writing!"

He stalked over with a ruler and began smacking my hands in a rage while I continued to pound the piano through a shaking dazzle of tears. Later I shut myself in my bedroom and whirled around in a fury, flinging pages and pages of my work in a white storm around me, sobbing and screaming, long after he had stomped downstairs to the basement and could not be reached, neither moved nor scared by my behaviour. I considered my writing to be the part of me that was beyond anyone's control, that could not be owned, the way I felt every other part of my body and my life belonged to my parents. My work was sacrosanct and inviolable. Anyone who tried to take any part of it away, who told me I was not allowed to write about this or that, called up a rage in me that was similar to the criminal lawyer's bottomless well. The lawsuit had transported me back to being the girl at the piano. To be told that I could not write something — a theme that continued all year, from the lawsuit, to worried editors passing my new work to lawyers for scrutiny prior to publication, to people prefacing their comments to me with the instruction that I could not write about what they were saying — baffled and angered me. In the mornings I sat wearily in the bathtub, the water cooling around me, thinking that I felt exactly like someone who hated her job, who dreaded going to work, whose dreary days of labour stretched ahead of her unbearably — as if I toiled in a factory, rather than at the sort of work people thought gratifying and rewarding. There seemed to be so many things you could not write about, stories you could not tell, dialogue you could not attribute; there were clauses in contracts about defamation and invasion of privacy, and disclaimers in books that said the characters and events came from the author's imagination and could not possibly have anything to do with anyone living or dead.

It occurred to me how easy it was to conjure a black cloud of dread when one is on the receiving end of a lawsuit. You are effectively robbed of months or years of ease and security, sentenced to sleepless nights. People who had never been sued before would experience as much worry as if they had been diagnosed with some rare illness that would require being subjected to a battery of invasive and time-consuming procedures over the next year. In *Lawyerland: What Lawyers Talk About When They Talk About Law*, Lawrence Joseph's intriguing, often excoriating non-fiction account of his conversations with lawyers and judges in New York, one criminal lawyer ranted, "'Why the secret? Why not just tell everyone? Every lawyer shall tell his or her client that becoming involved with the legal system is like three years of experimental chemotherapy, 100% guaranteed not to work.'"

In late June the editor and I met with our new lawyer at his large downtown firm to hand over the documents we had compiled. He was in his late forties, with sharply intelligent eyes and two lines parenthesizing his mouth. As we began discussing the case in his corner office I flushed, envisioning myself having to divulge in court some of the things I was now telling him, and muttered, "Oh my God, I'm going to feel like crawling under the table."

"Don't worry," he said dryly, "you'll have company down there."

He shook his head over the lawsuit, with its many embarrassing aspects. "This is not going to be a fun trial. Some trials are fun. This is not going to be one of them. It's too much like a matrimonial case" — and for the first time it occurred to me that the emotions involved made it resemble a divorce case more than a standard libel suit. Without that personal element, this lawsuit might have caused me hardly any turmoil at all; editors and journalists I knew who had been sued, sometimes often, barely paid attention to the claims, viewing them only as irritations. It was the relationship element of the case that had me in its grip.

A paralegal took the documents as we handed them over one by one, explaining the files and stacks of paper. Looks of discomfort descended over the faces around me when I talked about my sex life with Bill, and the lawyer said that he wasn't going to like it, but those details would be discussed in court, too. I looked around curiously, realizing I lacked a certain shame over things that other people regard as devastatingly personal. All I had to do was think of my time on the streets, the things I did in cars in back alleys, in deserted underground parking lots, in men's homes when their wives were away. When I thought of those things, everything else lacked the capacity to humiliate.

We ruminated for a while about Bill's possible motivations for bringing the suit, an irresistible but perhaps fruitless activity, since I was realizing that you could be so close to someone that you didn't know where they ended and you began, and yet later be no more capable of predicting their behaviour than someone meeting them for the first time. It was an odd feeling. I thought of him next to me in bed on sunny mornings, the warmth of his presence, how fervently we promised to protect each other.

The lawyer recited a list of documents to demand from the plaintiff — letters, press clippings, manuscripts. When I expressed my concern over the many letters I'd written to Bill, he sighed. "Don't ever put anything in writing." I thought what excellent advice that was, and how impossible for a writer — like the *New Yorker* cartoon in which Anaïs Nin's journals have been subpoenaed, and a man is wheeling them into the courtroom on dollies, stacks and stacks of them.

Outside, the sun was coming out, slant and silvery. After the meeting, as the editor and I walked down the street, I asked him what he would do differently if he could do it over again. He thought for only a moment. "Not too much. I'm still proud of your article." When I considered what I might have done differently, there were so many things in the relationship I could think of, and parts of the article I would have changed — mostly to make it a better piece of work — but I didn't regret the article itself either.

I still found myself unable to write. Whenever I went to my desk, the overwhelming defeat I felt expressed itself in three words that boomed in my head: "What's the point?" Someone else would hate me. Looking back, I thought there was never a time when I intended to hurt or betray anyone I wrote about; if it made for a good story, I simply had to write about it. Something literary and potentially lasting was of greater value to me than any relationship. As a child I believed I would never have any friends or relationships because of this, and that was all right. The writing burned in me, a singular obsession, worth every loss.

It had been a year since the relationship with Bill had ended, and I thought of how I felt during its last months — the misery that had washed between us, how trapped we had been in that crowded, claustrophobic space that had become the sum of us. Our relationship had become the world, a tight little whirlwind in which I had spun and spun. The lawsuit continued to keep me within its orbit, but at least I wasn't in its centre any more. I felt sadness for the good, close moments that had been lost.

The more I read about libel law, the more it looked like potential defamations lurked everywhere. If you wanted to, you could find negative imputations in all sorts of comments, and if that failed, you could always plead "innuendo" — that a phrase was defamatory in a sense other than its ordinary and natural meaning. "'When I use a word,' Humpty Dumpty said, in rather a scornful tone, 'it means just what I choose it to mean — neither more nor less.'" If only that were a defence in libel law! But it isn't; the writer's intention is considered irrelevant, since it is how the phrase might conceivably be understood by others that is important, even when the alleged meaning is not what the author meant. Still, people usually recognize that most incidents aren't worth suing over and voluntarily tangling yourself in the net of legal process. As more than one lawyer told me, "The plaintiff frequently ends up becoming the defendant in court."

During a lunch interview with a senior partner of a large downtown law firm, I mentioned what was beginning to feel like a serious loss of nerve whenever I approached my desk to write. "Oh, you mean libel chill," he said. I'd heard the term before, but it had not meant anything until now. I was itching to write about the lawsuit but he cautioned against that, because people involved in a matter before the courts who are viewed as seeking publicity or attempting to sway public opinion in their favour are frowned on by judge and jury. I protested that writing about my experiences was different from talking to the press.

"Do you think writing about something is more important than saying it?"

"Yes!"

He smiled. "So by writing about it, which is even more important, you'd be trying to do it even more."

It was a windy day; we were sitting outdoors, and the clouds flew across the sky. He had a brisk warmth, a genuinely solicitous manner that made him memorable to others I knew who had met him. When I asked him questions during the interview he spoke with measured caution, weighing every word, and I thought about how a lawyer's carefulness with language paralleled a writer's — the way both laboured over sentences before fixing them to the finished page.

"When you write a factum, you have to be accountable for every word," he pointed out. "In court, every word is subject to attack by the other side or the judge. You stare at the words, and you stare at the words, fiddling with commas."

He loved the law; it had been the driving force of his life. Others who knew him described him as having an incredible capacity for hard work, and as being a ferocious adversary in the courtroom.

"We take the law for granted because it's with us every day," he said. "It's a system of orderly, reasonable conduct — it provides rules by which a society is able to function. I know there is this negative, shystery image of lawyers out there, but most lawyers have a sense of honour."

He gestured at the bill on the table. "In a civilized society, law is a substitute for violence. Several hundred years ago, if we left without paying this bill, someone might chop off my hand. Now we have laws in place to handle that dispute in a reasonable fashion."

I refrained from saying that being sued nonetheless felt to me like a form of violence, a way for one person to strike at another by miring them in legal process.

"How old are you now?" he asked.

"Twenty-seven — just turned."

"Well then, you're still growing up, right? You might

be involved in another libel action when you're thirty-seven. And again when you're forty-seven. Say, one every ten years. So you might expect to be involved in three or four in your lifetime."

It was a harrowing thought. "If anyone wishes to be certain that he will not render himself liable to pay damages for libel. . . He would have to refrain from writing, printing or publishing or distributing any written matter of whatsoever nature," Peter Carter-Ruck wrote in *Carter-Ruck on Libel and Slander*. When I told the lawyer how this lawsuit had intimidated me, and that I was worried it would stop me from taking risks in my writing, he looked at me evenly.

"Well, that's the test then, isn't it?"

Increasingly it seemed to me that one of the defining issues of the day involved the right to privacy versus the public's right to know, particularly if you were a public figure. The talk shows, the kiss-and-tell memoirs, President Clinton's escapades and all those Americans who thought the media had no business exposing his sex life. Was there a backlash now, was public opinion favouring the life of privacy and dignity? As our first lawyer later pointed out to me, if we didn't already have telephone books and someone were to propose the idea of them today, people would be horrified: a book distributed to the public in which everyone's name, address and phone number would be published? In a paper on privacy torts, he wrote that "the dinner bell has been rung" in this area of litigation. What worried me most about this trend was that the public seemed unable to distinguish between confessional writing, which had always been part of literature, and the sort of breast-baring, fists-flying antics of the talk shows. It was all one and the same to them, and in many publications I read, even critics lumped together literary tell-all memoirs and talk-show behaviour, never mind what beauty of language and craft existed in the writing. Suddenly there was little difference between Kathryn Harrison's sensitively written memoir of incest, *The Kiss*, and the woman who appeared on afternoon television to sob and spill the details of her own experience of incest. Yet the most transparent veil of calling a piece of work "fiction," when it was known to all as being blatantly autobiographical and was even discussed in reviews as such, still often rescued a work from disapproval. In his novel *The Silent Cry*, one of

Kenzaburo Oe's characters says, "'Writers? . . . They deceive other people with a framework of fiction, but what essentially undermines the work of an author is the very fact that, provided one imposes a framework of fiction, one can get away with anything, however frightening, dangerous, or shameful it may be.'"

The prospect of eventually being in a courtroom before a judge intimidated me whenever I thought about it; I was afraid my anxiety would be so great I would barely be able to squeak monosyllabic responses. At the University of British Columbia Faculty of Law, a letter from a client to one of the Law Students Legal Assistance Program students, posted on the bulletin board, described her fear when she had to face the judge in court. She was so shaken she was almost unable to speak, and had been humiliated when he asked her if she needed an interpreter. ". . . I was overwhelmed with the seriousness of the situation. It was like when someone is being robbed and cannot move or yell or do anything."

I thought about the time I went for dinner at the house of a judge who was about to hand down a judgment the next day in a high-profile case. He invited me to come and watch if I wanted, so I went early the next morning. The glowering, silver-haired man in robes who swept into the courtroom while we stood in respect bore little resemblance to the man the night before at dinner, his shirt sleeves rolled up, later dancing in the living room with his chest thrust out to a comical children's song on the record player. When he handed down the judgment there was a moment of tense, wracked silence while the various parties tried to figure out what was going on, then disbelief and the thunderbolt of realization, the awful moment of comprehension. A bereft father stood up and began to bellow with grief and rage; he had to be carried out, shouting and flailing while the women cried. I held my breath, feeling uncomfortably like a voyeur to these people's pain, which lacerated the air. "But when you are beaten in the courts of law, there is a kind of dumb finality about it which I can only compare with the ultimate emphasis of death," Harold Laski wrote in his essay "My Day in Court." I looked at the man on the bench, his face impassive, though earlier he had read aloud a heart-rending victim's impact statement, to a soft wave of weeping, to validate the families' loss and provide them with some catharsis. I felt badly for him, almost wanted to protect him, yet he seemed quite emotionally detached from the drama of the people in his courtroom.

Why should I feel so intimidated by this other world? I remembered some of the lawyers who came to see me when I was a prostitute — the one who arrived on my doorstep straight from a lecture he had given to law students, carrying a briefcase full of whips and chains that he had kept next to him all night long, deriving a secret thrill from knowing its contents when his audience assumed there were only legal briefs inside. The one who engaged me in threesomes with his girlfriends, who took me on trips to a swingers' club for long evenings of group sex, his insatiable hunger for something more and different, underneath that his constant simmering rage that would sometimes erupt. The troubled one, puffy with alcohol and food, who was usually drunk and stumbling by the time I arrived; we would sit and drink morosely in his sunken living room with the leather-bound law texts surrounding the fireplace, I draped in his Queen's Counsel silks, while the ferries sailed back and forth on the blue water beyond the wall of windows, and later we would silently, sadly rock together on his bed. What had these men lost along the way? It's odd that what I experienced then, traipsing through those lawyers' elegant homes, should mean nothing now, should have nothing to do with this life, should fail to armour me.

In early October, the dates for examination for discovery were set for January. Now everything seemed real, cemented, and I could not stop that pulse of fear that leapt in me. All this time I'd been working to reconcile myself to the lawsuit, make it an ordinary occurrence in my mind, but when the lawyers' faxes spiralled out of my machine I still experienced a sickening lurch in my stomach. Whenever there was a new development, my heart would be squeezed by dread. My mind turned in tight circles, wondering what Bill could be thinking, feeling, what forces drove him. I hated every second he occupied my thoughts through the lawsuit, hated how careful I had to be when I was out socially and people asked me about the progress of the litigation. I would always wake the next morning worried that I had been my usual unguarded self and said too much. What was too much? What was an opinion based on facts versus provable truth? Should I not say anything that might hint at negative feelings, should I not admit to any human emotion except the most virtuous?

The strange thing was, at moments like these when my antagonism towards Bill should have been greatest, I instead felt acutely the loss, the utter unrecoverability, of the fine and tender moments that had existed between us. The travels through California, the diners and the heat, the gas stations and motels, the sun that lay over us and left us stunned. The contrast between the present and the past was so stark, like black shadows on a sunlit screen, that I thought I never wanted to risk being close to anyone again.

A journalist once asked if I regretted writing the article and I answered, perhaps too cleverly, that I regretted not having written a better article. As a piece of writing, now that I had some distance from it, I could see all its flaws and wished I could repair them. But I was asking myself that all the time — would I do it again, knowing the outcome? It was one of those useless questions that was nonetheless telling. I wasn't sure any more. I did value what I had learned so far, the way the lawsuit made me curious about a part of the world I had never noticed before. The difficult thing was the mystery of the process, how each development sent a

jolt through me because it was unanticipated and I had
nothing to compare it to, no way to guess its eventual
outcome. If I were a lawyer, it would merely be a job.

On a Friday afternoon I met a friend at her large downtown law firm before we went out for dinner. Prior to
the lawsuit I had never been interested in the work
that lawyers did; I had known this woman for years,
and had always assumed she was a criminal lawyer,
because I didn't know then that there was such a thing
as a civil litigator. It was late in the afternoon and she
was wearing jeans and sneakers, sipping a glass of wine
in her office with its shelves of heavy binders and view
of the surrounding office buildings. Traffic passed in a
silver stream below, heading for home. Other lawyers
wandered in and out of her office, preparing to leave
for the weekend. When I told her shyly that I was
thinking of applying to law school her reaction was
swift, forceful.

"You don't want to do that! No! You would hate it!
You don't want to become a lawyer!"

She sought confirmation from one of the other asso-
ciates on her floor, who shrugged. "It's okay. Except for

billable hours, senior partners, and clients." She laughed, gesturing at the flowers on her desk, which a client had sent. "Well, some clients."

On our way out to dinner we peeked into a room where a group of lawyers were gathered, in their dark suits, drinks in hand. "Those are the boring people," she whispered. "I can't imagine joining them. If you wanted to socialize with people from work, why would you stay at work? Why wouldn't you go out?" But from the doorway it looked like a party I wasn't invited to, the minds of the people inside turning with a knowledge that was mysterious to me.

I wandered through the Faculty of Law at UBC, with its crest above the entrance: "Let Justice Be Done Though the Heavens Will Fall." I looked at the students, wondering what they were learning that I didn't know, what knowledge filled their heads that was absent in mine. I had left school in grade ten and had so far been able to live my life by avoiding the academic structure that I loathed; but now, for the first time, I found myself feeling wistful. These people seemed so young and I had a hard time envisioning their future lives in court, in the glass box offices of a law firm. Here they were students gathered outside on the fall campus, eating lunch, digging for quarters at the pay phone, bent in solitude over books in the library.

In early November I attended two lectures on defamation at the Faculty of Law. It was the first time I had been in a classroom or lecture hall since I was a teenager, other than to give readings or attend writing workshops, and I loved it. My body was canted forward with interest the entire time. I arrived early and watched as the drab, windowless hall filled up with students — the mature students tending to favour the back seats, the noisy, laughing younger students charging in, eating muffins and carrying juice and coffee. It reminded me of high school, but it was different. When the lecture began a silence descended, and there was an almost audible hum of concentration in the air, pens dashing across pages, the soft, rapid click of keys on laptop computers. There were two young women in front of me who looked improbable as law students — they had long, tumbling blonde hair and wore provocative clothing. Their spandex tops were so tight I could see the outline of their bras. Were they smarter than I was? It seemed impossible that these students, many of whom looked so young, would in a few years write those intimidating legal documents, and handle serious, complex matters. I wanted what was already in their minds. In *The Lure of the Law: Why People Become Lawyers and What the Profession Does to Them*, Richard Moll found that many lawyers had been told from the time they were children that they should go into law, because of their ability to talk, to argue. Were they all going through a version of the emotional and intellectual journey Scott Turow chronicled in his first book, *One L*, a moving non-fiction account of his first year at Harvard Law School? He described reading his first case in law school as "something like stirring concrete with my eyelashes," and based on the reading I had done on defamation law, I could vouch for the accuracy of that description. Yet I wanted to stay forever. There were so many questions I wanted to ask, things I wanted to understand, but when I hurried down to the stocky, grey-haired professor at the end of the first lecture to thank him for letting me sit in, I was too embarrassed to do so — maybe they were stupid questions, the answers painfully obvious. As he was rushing out the door, a stream of students around him, I ventured that there were some contradictions in defamation law that confused me. He paused, interested, but then I stumbled and said, well, maybe it was just because I'd been reading British and American and Canadian law simultaneously and confusing them, though that wasn't it, and let him go. I couldn't shake the feeling that I didn't belong there, had no right to ask anything.

I met one of the mature students in first-year law, a woman in her late thirties who had dreamed of becoming a lawyer her entire life, and had made a number of sacrifices to be there now. She asked what I was doing there, and I told her reluctantly that I was being sued. Her face lit up, and before she could censor herself she burst out with an enthusiastic, "Oh, how exciting!" Later she apologized profusely, worried that she had been insensitive, but it made me laugh. She was exactly right. If only I could see the situation the way an aspiring lawyer might. Was it enough that I was starting to view it with the curiosity of a writer?

It was late November. The lawsuit was usually there, every day, in some small way — mostly when I was writing. Sometimes when I went to my desk there was a feeling of being unable to breathe, as if there were suddenly no oxygen in the room. I was in the final stretch of editing my new book, and I felt defeated by the slashing cuts that had been made over legal concerns. I felt as if I'd become like everyone else — afraid to take risks, concerned about lawsuits, creeping cautiously along hoping not to attract negative attention. The cuts represented the destruction of months of work, hundreds of days of turning over and scrutinizing every word before committing it to the page. Parts of the book seemed incomplete with those cuts — sadly lacking, bland and devoid of detail, now that certain scenes had been removed or diluted. I remembered reading about how Harold Robbins once got around the defamation laws in a novel that was clearly about Jacqueline Onassis by writing a scene in which the "real" Jacqueline Onassis made a cameo appearance. I seemed fundamentally unable to understand what my psychiatrist kept trying to tell me — that one's self was the most important thing one had, that to expose another's intimate self to the world could cause that person to wish to hurt me in whatever ways they were capable. I still expected everyone, including myself, to give that up for the writing, which was a higher purpose.

There were odd moments when I could vividly remember parts of the relationship with Bill — Palm

Springs, the sun, the sidewalks, the mall, the supermarket. The ordinary moments in the day, which in retrospect seemed poignant and bathed in a kind of intense light. It seemed a time of something like innocence, when this lawsuit would have been unimaginable. But now when he appeared in my dreams there was always a cruelty, a distance, there. Often he loomed larger than life, muscular and broad-shouldered, with a threatening, ominous physical strength. When he approached me I was never sure if he meant to kiss me gently or knock me down. When there was sex in the dreams, he was paying me for it; rage and contempt blazed on his face while I serviced him, maintaining the minimal amount of physical contact necessary for the transaction.

One day it occurred to me that the depression was over; it had been for a while. Yet I could not pinpoint the day, the hour, that the black shade lifted. It seemed to have something to do with seeing the lawsuit in a different light — through the observing eyes of a writer rather than the confusion of someone entangled in the process. The constant dread, the leaden mornings that accompanied litigation, shifted when I begin to look at it all as material, which was ironically how the article about my relationship with Bill came to be written in the first place.

It was mid-December, a year since the courier had shown up at my door with the letter from Bill's lawyer. I felt now that my life had opened up in some way and let in a part of the world I had never considered or observed before. In that sense, the experience seemed nearly worthwhile. I had some knowledge and curiosity about the law that I hadn't had a year ago, and this seemed to outweigh the anxiety, hurt, depression, and frustration that the lawsuit had brought.

At the round of Christmas parties and dinners, people would sometimes talk about my article and the lawsuit. Though their remarks were often in jest, I could see that they were newly cautious, leery around me; there was a look in their eyes as if there was something unpredictable or untrustworthy about me. I had an urge to leap up, wave my arms, and yell, "But I'm a good person! I'm kind and loyal and decent! Like me; love me!" When they asked me, yet again, "Why did you write that article?" I wanted to answer earnestly and thoughtfully, I wanted them to listen, and understand, but it was as though we were speaking different languages. The experiences that had brought us to this point in our lives were so divergent, our values and morals therefore so different, that I could not make them understand.

At one dinner party the couple next to me talked about the time they had been involved in a lawsuit. The husband had been sued by a woman in the service industry who claimed that he had struck her in the course of a disagreement; he said that he hadn't, that it was a set-up. His lawyer had advised him to give the woman a sum of money and settle, because it would be less expensive than going to court.

"I had always believed in the justice system until this happened," he said. It had infuriated him to settle, but he had followed his lawyer's advice, recognizing it to be the best course of action.

"The lawsuit was a black cloud that hung over us every day for two years," his wife said. "Every morning when we woke up the black cloud was there." She described how they had first walked into the lawyer's office "with leaden feet"; the last time they were in her office, settling the case, she could hear the lawyer's next appointment coming up the stairs. "They had that same leaden step. Clomp, clomp, clomp. They sounded exactly the way we did that first day. I felt for them; I understood their misery."

In the weeks before our examinations for discovery I was often distracted, brushing my teeth twice in a row, forgetting where I had put things. When I reviewed the chronological events of our relationship, the documents that our letters and articles and manuscripts had become suddenly seemed overwhelming. The dates and details, thrust under a microscope, were slippery, difficult to remember, to state as fact rather than as subjective, tricky memory.

The day of my discovery dawned grey and wet. The editor and I met our lawyer in his office, and we walked together to the court reporters' building, where we were told the meeting had been switched to another set of offices. The second floor of this other building was glassy and modern, with slanted walls and jewel-coloured furniture. The boardroom where we met had a strip of window, beige blinds, red chairs, and a plate of cookies in the centre of the table. Bill's lawyer came striding in with an associate from his office. He was sleeker than he looked on television, more groomed and fashionable than I had expected. His leather shoes shone with a soft, buffed glow beneath his well-cut suit. He sat opposite me and our lawyer sat next to me, and the two reached for cookies. I thought of how someone had described Bill's lawyer as not having a mean bone in his body, and when I'd mentioned that to our lawyer earlier, his mouth had crimped and he'd quipped, "And he's a lawyer?"

To our surprise, and my relief, Bill didn't show up. The court reporter placed the Bible in my right hand. "Do you swear to tell the truth, and nothing but the truth, so help you God?"

"I do."

It weighed awkward and unfamiliar in my hand. I fleetingly remembered a lawyer friend's weary observation that in most civil suits, both parties were somewhat to blame by the time they arrived at discoveries. "It's rare that either side is completely innocent of responsibility or wrongdoing," she had said.

As the questions began, I could feel myself drifting deeper inside myself to some quiet place. Our lawyer had worried about the impression my nervous laughter might leave, but the last thing that I felt like doing here was laughing. My voice came out in a whisper and I was still, as if everything in me had slowed down almost to a stop. Our lawyer took notes, black ink flowing in an elegant, illegible script across lined paper. I could feel his tense, alert energy next to me, the hum of his concentration as he listened to every word. When he objected to a question he was forceful and precise; Bill's lawyer maintained a look of amusement, leaning back in his seat, while his associate rapidly took notes throughout.

At the break we wandered through the area outside the boardroom, where there were chairs and glass tables and a long bar with coffee, water, and tea. Lawyers are not permitted to talk to their clients about their case during examination, to coach them in any way, so the editor, the lawyer, and I instead discussed the architecture of the building, as though nothing was happening. When I went to the bar to get more hot water for my tea, Bill's lawyer was there, and he gave me a little smile as he refilled his coffee cup. He seemed about to say something social to me, but our lawyer had followed me, wary, and he saw him and then said nothing.

There were more questions after the break, then Bill's lawyer had to go to court, so he left the rest of the questions to his associate. He strode quickly away in his long coat, a chocolate chip cookie in his hand — "Lunch," he said, waving it in the air. His associate had dark hair, dark eyes; she asked more questions about my sexual relationship with Bill, a subject the lawyer had been almost gentlemanly in approaching. I looked at her dispassionate face and wondered what she was thinking, if afterwards in the privacy of her home she would shake her head wearily over the day's allotment of sordid details.

Afterwards, we walked back in the grey drizzle, our lawyer smoking a cigarette, trying to figure out why Bill hadn't shown up. He praised my performance at discovery, smiling fleetingly at me, and this pleased me, as though the examination had been, after all, a kind of test.

The next day was the magazine editor's discovery. In the lawyer's office beforehand, while the two of them went over his answers to possible questions, the editor said in response to one of the questions that maybe they should go over the points one by one. Our lawyer sat back and gave his tight smile.

"No, not one by one. Never invite a lawyer for dinner, and never invite him to ask you more questions!"

Bill's lawyer was gregarious and charming in the casual conversation before the discovery began. Our lawyer was guarded with him, even in unrecorded conversation; in contrast, I thought Bill's lawyer was someone who wanted to be liked, who was surprised by our side's collective reticence and unwillingness to be engaged.

The mist and rain lifted for a while, and sunlight lay in bright, clean blades along the slats of the venetian blinds. Documents were shuffled, slapped on the table; papers were flipped back and forth in evidence binders. The associate who had again accompanied Bill's lawyer scribbled on a long legal pad, tearing out pages as she went, folding them, occasionally whispering to Bill's lawyer or passing a page to him. Her eyes looked tired, and I could see my female lawyer friends in her role, doing what she was doing, and it didn't seem like anything I wanted.

Afterwards, we all rode down in the elevator in a strained silence. The female lawyer, putting on her gloves, dropped one on my foot; I would have retrieved it for anyone else, but here that seemed like a concession, so I watched while she bent awkwardly to pick it up off my shoe. The doors opened finally and we went our separate directions in the deafening silence.

I woke up on the morning of Bill's discovery with a depression that had been absent before my own. The day was dark, raining. The editor and I hurried through a production crew's street filming — their bright white lights, equipment, and snaking cords — into the board-room. Bill, the lawyers, and the court reporter were already seated, waiting for us. I walked around the table to a chair at its end, feeling Bill's eyes on me, curious it seemed. It was a shock to see him, as though he were a character come alive. My heart pounded, and as the questions began I found it difficult to look at him. There were moments when I felt, for the first and only time, ashamed of certain passages in my article that, even though they were true, seemed ugly. I stared glazedly at the plate of cookies in front of me, the stack of paper napkins. Across the street, a curtain flapped in an open window of a hotel.

There were things I wanted to say to Bill that day that I could not, because of the lawsuit. I could have explained certain things, and he might have understood why everything turned out the way it did. But now any nugget of information could be used as a weapon, and the process of litigation prevented that sort of intimate, human disclosure. The most difficult thing about his discovery was that I had expected to see only the person who was suing me, not to see why I had been with him, something that had become almost unfathomable to me in the time since the relationship.

When it was over our lawyer stood up and the editor and I silently followed him. Bill's eyes were on me as I put on my coat; he was frowning. What was he thinking? His lawyer was moving papers around, packing them away; his face was tight, and he did not look at us. There was a feeling of the lawsuit drawing to a close, although it was impossible to predict what the other side would do next. As I walked out, Bill and I did not say anything to each other; it seemed we had learned that much, at least.

For several nights after the discoveries, I had intense, epic dreams about my family and childhood. But in a few days the grief was gone and in its place was the depression, the black curtain dropping down once again. A sense of deadness as I moved through the day, as if all feelings had been pushed into a sterile box buried deep inside me. Occasionally the fog was pierced by bright slats of memory — the safe, tender moments with Bill. It seemed that the hardest thing about attending his discovery was seeing that he was still the same person, that the people we had been were the same people we were in the room with the Bible and the lawyers and the court reporter tapping softly on her strange machine. This story was part of that story, and nothing could be relived or done over. The day of Bill's discovery would now always be part of our story, in which events changed beyond recovery, and maybe this one day was ultimately more memorable than the best of our time together. The time of the lawsuit might in the end eclipse the time we were close.

But within a week a thick tissue had grown over the wound that had opened. Already when I talked about the sadness, the loss, the memories, I could no longer feel any of it — they'd been buried again, or dissipated, that quickly. I realized to my surprise that I hadn't written down any of what I'd felt in the days following the discovery, that I had been in the full force of a genuine, unobserved emotion. Now I wanted to be able to catalogue those memories as a writer; they were so vivid, but they were almost gone. Bill squeezing my hand, gazing down at me in the flat California sunlight, the truck stops and motels, his reassurances that I could wake him if I got lonely (once, after the relationship had soured, I finally did; I wrote "I'm lonely," over and over with my fingertip, on his elbow, and he woke furious at me, anger swarming his features), the way we would lie in bed reading, my head on his stomach, his occasional happy glance in my direction, the way I would sleep for hours with my head on his shoulder. But even as I wrote those images down, they curdled. So many other things hadn't worked, and all I had been looking for in the relationship was a father. At the beginning Bill was adoring, attentive, yet I knew it would have to end if it were to duplicate my relationship with my real father. It would end because of my expression of my true thoughts, of what was really going on inside me. Once again I would have to give up that love and security, which were ultimately false because they were based on not saying what I thought or felt, in order to become myself.

"You didn't want a boyfriend. You wanted a daddy," Bill had said, his voice heavy, during our last telephone conversation. For a moment I was silent, astounded. How could he not have known that from the beginning? Like a child, I used to make him promise again and again not to lose me whenever I wandered away from him, in a store or a shopping mall in an unfamiliar city. But in the end I was lost.

On February 26, late on a Friday afternoon, our lawyer's assistant called. Her voice was bright — Bill had agreed to our counter-offer, which was simply to republish an apology on the letters page of the magazine, without paying his legal costs. The weather had been undecided all day — sun, cloud, rain, hail — but at that moment the sun shone, the sky was blue, and relief flooded through me. It was over. Yet it had been a part of me for long enough that I felt a curious numbness as well, a disbelief, as if some part of me had just been lopped off, but in its place a phantom pain continued.

So everything passed, but I was sure all of it left an impression, bright trails in the mind, like the streaks of comets in the sky. In the end, nothing much happened. But somehow, something changed. I learned things I hadn't known before — about relationships, about what can happen to love. I learned something about the law, and its practitioners; about the power of language, and the danger of words. For a brief time, a window opened on another world — the world of the law, which has its own indomitable process, its complex figures — and I looked in. It was only a small window, after all, and I wanted to see everything that passed by.

IN RESIDENCE

In 1994, I HAD saved enough money for a down payment on a condo, and it became my life's work to look for a place to live. This was not so easy — I was a self-employed twenty-two-year-old, the market was at its peak, and I could just barely afford an entry-level one-bedroom suite. Plus, I wasn't sure I was doing the right thing. Wouldn't any other young writer use those savings to travel the world, cataloguing her many adventures along the way? I wasn't even sure I wanted to stay in Vancouver, instead of moving to the United States or somewhere in Europe. It seemed that by putting down roots here, by assuming a $100,000 mortgage at a time when most of my peers were still living with their parents, I was sealing my fate.

But I wanted a home more than I wanted anything else. I wanted some semblance of security, of middle-class stability. The reason behind this was a deep, constant fear I have had since I was a teenager — a fear that I will someday once again be without a place to live, the way I was for a time in my adolescence.

I have lived alone — independent of my parents' home, group homes, and foster homes — since I was sixteen. I lived in a succession of basement suites and rented rooms, ones with spiders and cockroaches and bathrooms down the hall. It was a step up in the world for me to rent my first studio apartment in a real high-rise west of Vancouver's Main Street. I never thought of any of those apartments as home. Too often, they were places where I spilled alcohol on the carpets, took drugs, and tried half-heartedly to commit suicide. They were not refuges or private places, because they were also where I saw my "clients." The apartments themselves became, in my mind, as unbearable as what I was doing inside them.

I still equated the idea of "home" with my parents' house, so it had ugly connotations for me. "Home" was a place from which I continually had to escape — if no longer physically, then in my dreams at night. During the day I would expend vast amounts of energy to avoid thinking about my family, but at night I had countless dreams set inside their house. I would recall every detail of that Vancouver Special — the pattern of the shower and kitchen floor tiles, the warp and weft of the living room carpet. I would be dreaming about some mundane event that had happened the previous day, or perhaps about something that was troubling me, and it would play itself out within my parents' house. It was so obvious, time after time, that it was disappointing — was my subconscious as simplistic as that? I longed to one day stage my dreams in another setting.

I became consumed with looking for a home of my own. Over the course of a year, I looked at nearly fifty apartments, and spent many hours seeking advice from friends and paging through *Real Estate Weekly*. Everyone had different opinions about what I should do. "You can't lose with real estate." "If you buy at the peak of the market, it can only crash." "Vancouver isn't going to get any smaller, it's only going to get bigger." "I have one word for you: 1997."

When I confessed my fear of homelessness to Brian Fawcett, a Toronto writer who had been a city planner, he said, "If you buy now, you'll have more chance of ending up homeless than if you keep renting."

But I persisted. Finally I did find an apartment, a 650-square-foot one-bedroom suite, and moved in days before my twenty-fourth birthday. It isn't much, but it has turned out to be one of the best things I have ever done for myself. It is my responsibility, my solace, and my shelter. I am attached to it with the sort of passion that one normally reserves for love affairs. When I am away from home, which is more and more often, I bore people at dinner parties by drawing floor plans of my suite and asking them what interest rates they have locked in at and for how long. I love to talk about real estate because, quite frankly, other than literature it is the only thing I know anything about. I miss my apartment when I am gone, and go over its humble attributes in my mind for reassurance.

I have an efficiently laid out one-bedroom suite with an enclosed balcony that I use as an office. The rooms are modern and angular, with light walls and carpets, and marble tiling in the entrance and the bathroom. The windows are double-glazed, and I have splash tiles above my kitchen counter. Each of these things gives me a pleasure I can hardly convey. Sometimes in the evenings when things are quiet, I walk around my home touching its walls and cupboards and windowpanes. I am able to tell it that I love it in a way I might not dare tell another human being. Look — I have a garburator, a self-cleaning oven, a dishwasher, a washer and dryer! These are all firsts, and they belong to me.

True, it doesn't have any of the features I would have liked in my first apartment — no high ceilings, hardwood floors, or spiral staircase (I will have arrived when I have that spiral staircase). I could actually be renting it for less than what I am paying in monthly mortgage installments. With my luck it will be impossible to sell and I will have to end up taking a loss for it. But for the first time in my life I no longer think of my estranged parents' house as my "home." "Home" is what I have chosen for myself, the tiny space I have carved out in urban Vancouver.

Sometimes I wonder if I will ever be able to give it up, this small abode, this my first place in the world. I know how difficult it must be for people who have not had to struggle to secure their first homes to understand the way I feel. "What's the big deal?" Certainly there are people who buy and sell houses and apartment with utter nonchalance. There are people who purchase their homes over the phone. I wonder what these people are like in the rest of their lives.

Of course, being avaricious and seldom satisfied, my head still turns at Open House signs the way a man's might at a pretty girl passing by on the street. I have become addicted to the real estate channel on television, and the first thing I do upon finding myself in a hotel room in another city is to locate this channel and spend an eye-glazing hour or so watching static pictures of houses and apartments cycle by on the screen, accompanied by the soothing voice of the realtor listing their fine attributes — cathedral ceilings, soaker tubs, marble entryways. I often yell aloud with envy or outrage. I moan at the vision of mansions I will surely never live in. In Winnipeg or Saskatoon, on some leg of another book tour, I manage to thoroughly depress myself by seeing that I could have bought a house with what I paid for my 650-square-foot apartment in Vancouver.

When a friend and I drive down Point Grey Road, ostensibly to enjoy the view after a movie or dinner, I grip the window frame and crane my neck to view the lofty houses and condominiums passing by. *What lives must their owners live?* I ask myself. Surely their every moment must be spent in grace and happiness. I know it can't be true but sometimes, like a child, I still think this. It is always a minor agony for me to take a taxi to the airport, past the sprawling houses of Shaughnessy.

My heart aches with the envy I feel. For many years I have nursed the fantasy of walking up to a beautiful house I've admired, ringing the doorbell, and inviting myself into the lives of the people who reside there. How could they refuse my winning demeanour?

Someday, I think I would like to live in such a house. I have always been intrigued by what takes place behind those front doors with their knockers and stone lions, that picket fence with its latched gate. I have a fierce desire to be on the inside, looking out. I remember being fourteen years old and walking around Burnaby all night after I'd run away, watching the light dawn over the green lawns of the slumbering homes. And Port Coquitlam, and East Vancouver, and Kerrisdale — I watched the sun rise over all those neighbourhoods. And I thought that what happened inside those houses — the husband getting dressed for work, the wife in her bathrobe, the children crunching toast — I thought that what happened inside must be the most heart-wrenchingly beautiful thing of all, the drama of daily life, of connectedness between people, and of the security they had earned for themselves. I thought that if I ever survived, that would be what I would seek for myself.

THE DREAM OF THE
PURPLE DRESSER

ONCE, A FEW YEARS ago, I went for a walk in the neighbourhood in which I grew up. Past the elementary school, the drugstore where I'd been caught shoplifting, the house where a certain boy used to live, downhill towards my former home. The trees were leafier, the houses roomier and more attractive, than I remembered them. It was a summer afternoon, the sky untroubled, the air dusted with pollen. My unhappy memories had made everything seem shrunken and ugly, and by comparison the streets were like boulevards, vast and light-filled. But my chest tightened as I came within blocks of the house that had appeared relentlessly in my dreams over the past ten years. In the distance a small, middle-aged Chinese woman came towards me, grocery bags weighing down her thin arms. My parents had moved away from this neighbourhood years ago, and I watched incredulously as this woman who looked like my mother came closer and closer. Could it be? In a moment the past decade vanished, and I was back inside the small world of that neighbourhood, circumscribed by the school and the grocery stores and the house in which I had lived. There was nothing else. Downtown was an image of clustered buildings on the horizon, glittering at night. It might as well have been on another planet. It was as if I had stepped through a veil into another world, the parallel universe of the imagination, the one in which everyone lives out their lives the way they would have had they made one choice instead of the other. I watched with dread as the woman with the lined face and the severe look in her eyes crossed the street and came within steps of me. I expected her hand to grasp my arm like a claw, to be dragged back to that house where, in my mind, the drama was still being played. I should never have come back, never stepped through the veil into the old world with its magical hold over me. But this woman who could have been my mother walked right past me, continued on her way, and the black spell was broken.

I circled the house. It belonged to another family now, with their own daily tribulations, their private crises, their moments of gratitude and peace. They had changed its look with a swing set, a satellite dish, and toys in the front yard. It appeared untidy, the way my mother would never have allowed it to look. But still I expected to see the faces of my parents in the living room window, and indeed my own face pressed against the rectangle of the bedroom window, round and pale and desperate. In my mind I would be there always, would always leave a part of myself behind in that place no matter how far away from it I tried to go. I found I could only walk past that house on the opposite side of the street, as if venturing any closer would pull me into its magnetic field, and I would be swallowed whole by the past.

In dreams, the protective filters fall away and the parables and metaphors are as clear as primary colours. It is a child's logic that reigns in this nocturnal world, where nearly every dream takes place inside the structure of my parents' house. The people in my life now, the situations that currently cause unrest, duplicate themselves and their dramas there. How I have gone over that house's every detail as obsessively as my mother might have done, crawling on her hands and knees along the length of the carpet to gather in her palm any stray hair or crumb of dust the vacuum might have missed! In trying so hard to forget, to deny that other life, I have remembered everything, and it all comes out at night. The lights go up in that locked theatre, and every inch of that set has been faithfully reproduced.

Sometimes I dream of running away again, violent dreams in which I race through the house, heart pounding, gathering everything necessary — my diaries, money, toiletries. It is like having only minutes to pack for an overseas journey; I am forgetting all sorts of important things. I try to leave through the kitchen door, but the stairs have vanished and it is a long and dangerous drop to the ground. Then I try to escape through the basement, into the garage, but it is dark and labyrinthine down there, with locks and bolts that can't be unfastened. There is always only the one way out, the way I actually left — through the front door. Almost sobbing with desperation, I rummage through the rows of shoes by the entrance, looking for a pair that will fit, a practical pair of shoes in which I can walk and run for the weeks and months to come, but I can't get the laces tied, or I can't find the other shoe, or all I can salvage is a pair of slippers. My parents are coming now, their footsteps thudding down the stairs. I have to unlock the heavy wooden door, my fingers fumbling, as in a horror movie when the axe murderer's shadow is already falling across the girl's shoulder while she is still trying to unlock the damn door in order to escape. Finally I fall into the bright air of the neighbourhood, and run. I run breathless from my parents' house, only it is more like awkward striding, because suddenly the air has turned thick and gelatinous. I lift and lower each leg with tremendous effort, and barely get halfway down the block. The whole time I am, shockingly, screaming obscenities at my parents at the top of my lungs. Always at this point I wake up, my throat hoarse as if I had actually been shouting in my sleep, my heart slamming in my chest, with the sinking knowledge that after all these years a part of me still lives in that moment when things were torn apart.

The dream I have most often, sometimes several nights in a row, involves an ugly lavender dresser that dominated my bedroom when I was growing up. One day the neighbours had tried to cart it away to the dump, but my thrifty parents had intervened and rescued it for my room. Its paint was peeling, its drawers creaked and would only open after several valiant tugs with one's entire body weight thrown in the other direction, and after years in my possession its every surface was scarred with stickers and scrawls. In the dream, this dresser is sitting in my current apartment. I cannot get rid of it, this baggage from the past. I loathe this eyesore, but my dream self believes that calling the movers or the Salvation Army will do no good, no one will be able to lift it and carry it away. I stare at it, walk back and forth in front of it, try to push at it, but it will not move an inch. To my despair, it is here to stay.

There was another house we lived in for the first six years of my life. It was old, covered in stucco and bits of rock and glass the colour of beer bottles, which I invariably scraped an elbow or a knee against when I passed on the narrow path. It had a bay window, scuffed hardwood floors, and a backyard where my mother grew corn sweeter than any to be found in supermarkets and honeyplums whose yellow skins split from the heavy nectar and flesh inside. I spent long hours riding a pink plastic dog with orange handlebars, my feet kicking and pedalling. Here we had moments of peace, placid days when we were thankful for the abundance that was ours. Several of my aunts lived with us off and on while they accumulated the funds to move into their own houses and lives and marriages, and they seemed sweet to me, feeding me forbidden jelly candies sprinkled with sugar, their youngish faces lit with smiles. One was beautiful; she wore blue eyeshadow that made her eyes look huge and went out on dates with nervous, eager men who gave me presents in an effort to seal their places in her life. My father taught me to ride a bicycle, and somewhere in a dusty photo album there must be pictures of us captured forever, my little legs pedalling, one of his large, veined hands on the handlebars, then the smile and pride on his face when he could let go and I wouldn't fall. In those pale folds of memory his face is still smooth — all of their faces are smooth and smiling — and I realize that my parents were the age of many of my friends today, and the hope they must have had wrenches my heart.

I remember other photographs — me wearing a puffy jacket with a furry collar from which my face and hands barely protrude, looking like a little snowman; me at the fair, holding a cone of candy floss nearly as tall as I was. How many of these memories are authentic, and what has been distorted by time? I can't trust that anything happened the way I remember it. But there are flashes of memory so banal yet insistent that they must have happened. I remember eating baby food from a jar at the kitchen table years after I should have been, and loving its comforting texture, no need to chew, only to open my mouth passively. I remember the honeyplums, bouncing like miniature suns in the wet colander placed at the centre of the table. Plenitude. The game where I would tell my mother to shut her eyes and open her mouth for a big surprise! — and into her trusting face I would pop a malted milk candy from the Horlick's jar in the fridge, of course sneaking one for myself in the process, until she grew irritated and snapped, "Enough!" I remember our neighbours: on the one side a couple who fought, shouting and banging through their house for the whole block to hear, how coarse the woman looked and how she wore too much makeup; on the other side a family who had a girl who was my friend, though she was older, maybe even a young teenager. How proud I was that I could spell Mississippi and she couldn't! And the long days of exquisite boredom, when I must have done nothing but played, and learned to read, and ineffectually helped with chores.

Those first few years seem unblemished next to all that followed, and yet I remember the dark things, too. One of my aunts suddenly shouting and smashing dishes during dinner; the phone calls we would get from the psychiatric ward after she had been picked up in the streets or on a bus. How I would be ushered out of the room in the sudden, strained silence, weighted with sadness. Is it my imagination or did we continue to use for some time a Thermos that was chipped from her throwing it against the wall, and I was fascinated by the spiderweb crack, the bits of silver and plastic that went missing in that violent episode? I remember my mother washing me in a basin, choking with an incomprehensible adult grief that bewildered and worried me. I remember my parents' fights, my mother's voice rising hysterically in the bedroom down the hall, my father's low and trying to be reasonable; how he would come into my bedroom and try to console me when I began crying, and how my mother would stalk in, her face deathly white in the light from the window, mocking us both, saying she would leave me and then who would look after me? I cried and cried. It is that moment I remember more than any other, how danger-ous and frightening her face had looked, the terrible power she had of taking everything away. And it must have been then that I began to worry myself sick over losing my father, that I began to develop all kinds of prayers and incantations, which I recited for many hours late into the night, trying to keep him safe from men who might beat him up on the streets and sicknesses that might befall him, trying to keep him safe from my mother whom I was convinced would some day destroy him. The anxiety I felt over the next few years was unbearable, and I could not share it with anyone. Perhaps it all began there, the pattern of my life and my relationships — the married men and their wives with whom I must continually duplicate that one story, the original story. The older men and their wives who are father and mother, and losing my father over and over again to the other woman in the bedroom at the end of the hallway.

There was a game my mother and I used to play. In this game she would line up all my stuffed dolls and animals on the back of the sofa, and I would clamber up and seat myself somewhere in that lineup, not much bigger than the toys on either side of me. She would pretend to be walking past on a city street, peering into the windows of shops along the way for something to purchase and take home. She would look into the window at all the pets and dolls lined up inside, and exclaim to herself about which one was the cutest, which one she would most like to have. I would try to look especially cuddly, so she would pick me. Part of the game, part of its exquisite torture, was that she would pick up the other dolls first, one by one, cooing over them, debating which one to buy, weighing each one's redeeming qualities, while I would pout and pretend to cry, kicking my feet against the back of the sofa, trying to draw attention to myself, the cutest doll of all. I would wait, grieving, tense with excitement, nearly exploding with it, all my self-worth balanced on the head of a pin. She would even go through the motions of purchasing one of the dolls, cradling it admiringly in her arms and sauntering off with it down the imaginary sunny cosmopolitan street. Then I would really holler — overcome with a jealousy that was partly delicious, partly painful — and she would eventually take pity on me, retrace her steps, toss the other doll carelessly aside, and scoop me up in her arms. I never tired of this game. The feelings that burst in me when she chose me above all the others were incomparable, so sweet that they were well worth the waiting and wondering, in fact were fuelled by it. Had she chosen me right away, the game would not have been half as interesting. It was how she drew it out like a strand of taffy, made me suffer, at times made me wonder if I would ever be noticed, ever be ultimately chosen. There were times, I suppose, when she didn't choose me, and I would begin to cry, even though I knew it was a game, until she gathered me in her arms.

By the time I was six I loved words, books, language; whenever children were called to the front of the classroom to struggle through a passage in a book, I was eager for my turn, to feel those words in my mouth, translated from the page to sound, to story. The mouth feel of words was as delicious as sugar and fat. They seemed to have shapes, and colours, and textures — a rainbow of possibilities. They were bristly and clunky or round and smooth, soft and puddly or hard and boxy. I already knew then that I was going to grow up to be one of those people who put words down on the pages of a book. I could think of no other purpose for the life that lay ahead of me. I could think of no higher aspiration, no worthier goal, than to give to others the tickly excitement of reading, to fill their minds and hearts and imaginations with people and stories that bloomed in them, grew inside them and became real to them, all from black letters marching across a page. Yet I wasn't obsessed with it the way I would be later. For years I thought I would write mysteries, science fiction, romances — books intended to give pleasure, to transport their readers into another reality, another realm. I wanted to give to others what I felt there in that classroom, tucked into my seat, opening a book with rapturous anticipation, gardens and friends and bicycles blossoming in my mind.

I was the child who stayed after school to help the teacher clean the blackboards — it was considered an honour, somehow — and whose assignments were littered with glittery stars and stickers. Shy, introspective, and bruisingly sensitive, I was probably seen as just another smart Chinese kid, the way all Chinese children are supposed to be: obedient, never causing trouble, a high achiever by parental demand if not by nature. I adored my teacher, a plump middle-aged woman who wore polyester. She could be stern, which made her praise all the more worthy.

One day my mother clipped a bouquet of hydrangeas from the bushes at the side of the house for me to bring to my teacher. The blooms were huge, violet and pink and blue, composed of clusters of butterfly-shaped petals; they were my favourite flower. The teacher exclaimed over them, arranged them in a vase, and displayed them on a table. Sometime that morning, while we were all quietly engaged at our desks, she called to me.

"Bring me those beautiful flowers, dear. I want to have them on my desk."

I stood up and walked over to the bouquet. I was often terribly anxious because I wanted to please, and was so afraid of doing something wrong. Whenever my parents told me to walk over and pick something up, perform some kind of chore or duty, anxiety would surge in me until I could not think. I was terrified of doing it wrong, of going in the wrong direction, of being yelled at, put down. Instructions were important; I listened to them and followed them to the letter. She had not told me to bring the vase, only the flowers. I proceeded to lift the unwieldy blossoms out of the glass vase, struggling to keep them together in my arms, and when I had them all I walked towards her. The stems dripped and dripped across the carpet. She stared at me, incredulous, furious.

"How stupid can you be! I can't believe what a stupid child you are! Put them back in the vase and sit down!"

She then called on someone else to clean up the mess I had made, honoured another child with bringing the flowers — this time in the vase — to her desk. I sat there bitterly ashamed and bewildered. She had asked me to bring her the flowers. When I had presented the flowers to her before class, they had not been in a vase; how could I have known that was what she had meant? At home, instructions were expected to be followed without deviation, in order to avoid reproach, and that was what I had tried to do. Up to that day I had loved this teacher, worshipped her. Now what we had had between us, that fragile thing, was broken. Nothing was ever the same again between us. I had loved her, in an oddly passionate way, and then she had hurt me, and I had had to stop loving her. I've never forgotten the humiliation of that day, the sensation of an attachment being severed.

Attachment. What happens when that is damaged? When the prospect of attachment becomes a threat, because it has always meant a loss of self, giving up all independence? For years I must have thought that if I could sever the tie to my parents, then nothing else I did could possibly be worse. Really, what could compare to that? I had run away from home, from my Chinese family; nothing else mattered. It felt sometimes like committing a murder. Everything else is so slight as to be laughable after that. Once you've stepped over that line — crossed from one moral world into another — you look back at the old world with its rules and etiquettes and codes, spoken and unspoken, in a kind of bemused, detached way. You're amazed that any of it could matter now, that any of it could be strong enough to hold you in, contain your behaviour. You step over one line, then another, and soon you're someplace else entirely where no one can reach or follow you. It's so easy. I had to do it over and over; it offered a strange, temporary relief. If all it took was one morning when you walked out the door and kept walking and just never went back — and the air parted obediently before you, not like in dreams, where it held you back, weighed down your limbs, grew heavy like mud while your parents ran after you — then what couldn't you do? Who else couldn't you walk away from, injure, betray? All that was nothing by comparison. If your own parents proved so ineffectual that they could not even stop you from hurting yourself, how could anyone else hope to hold you down?

Some of us try for most of our lives to return to that beginning, or to deny and destroy it. "Ding dong, the witch is dead," a friend of mine said with a hard look in his eyes when his father was diagnosed with a terminal illness. I remember men who told me that they couldn't wait for their fathers to die so they could flush their ashes down the toilet. This is the beginning of all hatred, all desire and love. One night, over dinner with a friend's new girlfriend, she described eloquently how much she loved her father and the close relationship they had. "Even when I was nineteen, I would sit watching television with my head in his lap." She described in wonder how, before she had met my friend, she had never felt with any man the safety she felt with her father. "When he hugged me for the first time," she said of my friend, "I felt completely enclosed. It reproduced those same feelings I had with my father." Her slim hands shaped a capsule in the air, and she shivered a little with the remembered good feeling, the astonishment of it. She was not someone who had spent her life searching for a father figure — her father was still alive, they were still close — but the attachment that she had experienced only with him was what she had sought with other men.

Sometimes my desire for family, for a father, is so great that it consumes me. When I try to wrench a man I perceive to be a father figure away from his family, and he doesn't comply — of course, if he did comply, he would quickly stop seeming suitable as a surrogate father — I plummet into a cauldron of self-loathing. Once I would have turned tricks, taken drugs, cut myself, to bury the feelings of worthlessness that come flooding out. Now I more or less try to endure them, during weeks or months when colour is bleached from the world and I have to fight not to be pulled under by each wave as it towers in the sky and then crashes down. During those times it is difficult to conceive of feelings as things that are contained inside us, generated by us, rather than as wild exterior entities that batter our small selves. Food can take on a hysterical, monumental significance. I can't get enough of it to fill the vacuum that has opened up inside me. A stranger will walk past on the street, casually munching a donut or a bag of chips, and I will grit my teeth in rage. It rises and rises inside me, choking me.

My father liked certain foods, which I remember still: banana chips, Almond Roca, the pope's nose on a chicken. They were among the foods my mother restricted him from eating, though he was slim and wiry and had no need to be on the diet she imposed on the whole family in an effort to make me lose weight. To this day I cannot encounter any of his favourite foods without tears stinging my eyes. I will stand in the candy aisle of the supermarket, fighting back sobs at the thought of the sweets and fats he liked but was not allowed to have, these small morsels of pleasure he was denied. All because of me, I still think. I remember how slowly he ate, savouring his food; I remember a party where the other men teased him because they were going back for seconds while he had barely made a dent in the plate of food balanced on his knee, surely liking it so much he had no need to gorge, to get rid of it as fast as possible the way I had begun to do, swallowing every forbidden forkful in a burning, shameful haste. Even now, when I allow myself to purchase some desirable sweet — a package of cookies, a cake, a container of ice cream — I will have to eat it all in one panicked binge, and then run to the bathroom with grief welling up inside me like nausea and force a toothbrush down my throat. Even now, the plush mouthful of chocolate cake is the last bite of food I have stolen from my starving father, yet I cannot help stealing it, the need for it is so much like the need for love.

More than anything in the world, when I was a child I wanted to protect my father. How I dreaded the weekends when we went to Chinatown to shop for groceries, passing through the bleak strip of skid row to reach the colourful markets and the crowds. I would spend hours lying awake the night before, praying fervently that he would not be hurt by the street people who lurched past us, the alcoholics and homeless with their bruised, weathered faces and stained clothes. I was convinced that one day it would happen — one of these men, who mumbled or yelled incoherently at us as we passed, would take a wild swing at us, and my father would try to defend us. I pictured him bloodied, broken, sprawled dead on the pavement. The weekends were unendurable. I spent most of the week worrying about our next foray into Chinatown, those few blocks we would have to traverse to get there. It was a lifetime's journey, my fierce praying as a bum staggered past, the blinding whiteness of the pavement, my anxiety at that moment so extreme that the world seemed to tilt and crack open and everything seemed to burst with light. There was my small, thin Chinese father, with his plastic glasses and prominent Adam's apple, and I don't know how many times a bum veered in our direction, muttering, exhaling cooking-wine fumes, and my heart stopped because I thought this was going to be the end. My father would be snapped in two like a match, and there was nothing I could do to stop it.

When I was thirteen I volunteered at a weekly community newspaper. Too young to doubt my abilities as a writer and journalist, I churned out profiles, news stories, play reviews, as well as learning the workings of the small office. I had come to the rather practical conclusion that I would make possible a career writing books by also writing for newspapers. To see my words in print, under my byline — it was as good as anything, worth the shyness I had to overcome to interview someone.

One afternoon I stayed late to meet a deadline, and then was delayed going home because it was winter, snowing, and the buses were running slowly. I arrived home just before dinner, and my mother was white-faced with fury. It had become difficult to predict her moods; I never knew what expression would greet me when I opened the door, whether she would be warm and cheerful or bitter and enraged. I would often return home with my heart suspended in my throat, dread churning in my stomach. Her face that evening was chalky in the dim light as she demanded to know where I had been.

Our drama that evening was finally interrupted when my father came home. Immediately we each tried to pull him to our side — my mother ordering him to punish his lying, whoring, ungrateful, uncontrollable daughter; I trying to tell him why I had been late through violent sobs. And wasn't he late himself that night? Why couldn't he tell her that the buses were running slowly because of the weather? Tell her! I wonder what he felt, that evening, caught between two hysterical, furious women. I wonder if he thought that life had not brought him what it had seemed to prom-ise, years ago, when we were in the other house and he was teaching me to ride a bicycle around the block, when at seven I was judged smart enough by the teach-ers at my school to be promoted from grade one to grade three, when he spent his days at work instead of going from one job interview to another. I wonder if he felt that life had let him down, that the summer had passed into a winter from which he would never emerge.

My father came into my bedroom and stood in front of me. I was sitting on the bed, hunched over, sobbing. I had been crying for hours and couldn't stop; I felt as if my insides had been torn out and my throat had turned to sandpaper. I wanted him to defend me. All this time, these battles between my mother and I that he missed or chose to ignore, pretended not to see — all I wanted was for him to defend me. He had come into my bedroom when I was small, when my mother was threatening to leave us, and extended his hand to comfort me. He had stayed with me in the darkness — we had taken each other's side, according to my mother, who stormed out, defeated, because it was him I called for, him I wanted, and because he would not leave me. But he couldn't defend me any more; he wasn't willing to. He stood in front of me. I did not look up at him. I wonder what he saw — a pudgy adolescent girl in cast-off clothing, with limp hair and a face distorted and ugly from hours of crying. What was he supposed to do with this ungainly person? I was, horribly, his. He was supposed to look after me, and he couldn't. All he could do was tell me to study hard, get good grades, help around the house, and listen to my mother. Punish me when I didn't do the above. All he could do was keep a roof over our heads and food on the table, and he hadn't even been able to do that for years.

I could hear him breathing in front of me. For a while he said nothing as I cried. We could both hear my mother, muttering bitterly to herself, occasionally erupting in a loud diatribe against me. Exhausted, I pleaded with him again to reason with her. His face, when I looked up, was dark, weary, and filled with discomfort. I could see that he was angry with both of us for putting him in this impossible situation. "She's your mother," he said shortly. "Even if sometimes she might not be right, you have to listen to her." Then he turned around and left the bedroom, went downstairs as he always did now, possibly to get away from us. It was true, then — he could no more protect me against my mother than I could protect him against the drunken men in the street. I continued crying for a while, but a curious numb calm had spread inside me. It was all over, and in that moment of abandonment I did not know which of my parents I hated more.

Those moments when we fall out of love with someone are so small. The other person may not even be aware of it. He may just be going about his day, doing what he thinks is right, but suddenly he has become lost to you forever. All because of a look, a gesture, the wrong word spoken at the wrong time. From that moment on I saw clearly that my father was incapable of protecting me. He would never again choose to comfort me, even when it meant I would have to endure my mother's wrath. We were each on our own now, planets rotating around each other in the house.

But in a wedding photo of my parents that wavers in my memory, their faces are sleek and young, their skin plump and unlined, light breaking across their eyes. My mother holds a bouquet of plastic flowers, because she considered real ones to be an unjustifiable extravagance.

Looking back, it is also the smallest moments that seem to radiate the most pain. The moments when you realize you loved these people, helplessly, that you were given no choice in this matter of loving them, and that they will always be part of you no matter how you try to carve them out of your flesh. That you are tied to them with bonds you could never sever, that they will live on inside you no matter how many effigies of them you hang and burn, no matter how often their reflections appear in the eyes of other men and women, men and women who then unwittingly play the roles of father and mother, with whom you act out the drama again and again.

I remember my father carrying glasses of Coke into the living room on the rare occasions we had company. My mother would spend hours and hours making traditional Chinese snacks and sweets, which would be heaped in plates on the coffee table. They both tried too hard. They seemed to carry around the feeling that they weren't good enough, that they were less than other people, certainly less than white people. It is a conviction that has leaked into me, one I battle with in my interactions with others. Imagine walking around in a world where everyone you see, everyone who brushes past you, is superior to you. All because of the colour of their skin. I have to try to hide the natural deference that rises in me, choking me like gall.

They had few friends, all of whom were Chinese, and having company was an occasion. I see my father carrying the soft drinks in from the kitchen, the black liquid sparkling in the glass tumblers. He would have to walk very slowly because he had filled the glasses to the rim. The Coke was virtually lapping at the lips of the tumblers. My mother snapped at him afterwards — why did he fill the glasses to overflowing like that? Was he trying to cause an accident? But I looked at his face when he walked in with the drinks, and I knew. He was trying to be good enough, that was all. I saw the anxiety to please, the desire to give, the pleading not to be put down. These emotions wrestled nakedly in the muscles of his face, his shy, darting eyes, his nervous grin. He walked forward towards the strangers in his house, defenceless, holding out everything he had.

I think there were moments when something different than what I remember existed between my mother and myself. There must have been. A look on her face, a light in her eyes. An afternoon when I was small, and she let me greedily go through the drawers in her bedroom, handle the astonishing booklets of thin papers matted with powder that were meant to be pressed to the nose, the jade jewellery, the pretty, softly bristling sweaters of beaded cashmere or lambswool that she had packed away in plastic because she considered them too good to wear. I remember the light in the south-facing bedroom, dust motes hanging golden in its path, the deep mystery of her past that tickled my nostrils like perfume. She would tell me how beautiful she had been as a young woman, with a glossy black mane so thick it could not be contained in a single braid and skin like apple blossoms, pink and white. I somehow understood that it was not age but the responsibilities and hardships of having a family, which she took so seriously it made a martyr of her, that had in her eyes robbed her of her beauty. She still had unusually white skin and large, light brown eyes, but her hair had begun to thin, and she had lost several of her teeth, so that when the doorbell rang unexpectedly she would make a mad dash through the house to insert the false teeth that wavered pinkly in a glass of water in her bathroom. It was one of the few displays of vanity that remained from her youth, and whenever I witnessed that panicked race through the house I saw her, for just a moment, not as my mother but as a woman concerned with her appearance, and for a moment it made her vulnerable and real.

Somewhere in our daily battles there must have been moments when we laid down our arms and regarded each other as allies. Moments of relaxed silence, when her tense face softened and the driven, desperate look left her eyes. I have to strain to remember them, to recall a mere handful. They did not last long, these small spots of calm, but they did allow me hope. Outwardly there was the clean house, the car in the garage, the orderly neighbourhood — the hope that perhaps these things and everything they symbolized could be sustained.

How did others see them, this mother and this father? Two small people in the world; two scrawny, poorly dressed Chinese immigrants with no power over anything? Yet they were huge in my mind, terrifying in their ability to injure with the slightest word or gesture. I could not see them as they surely appeared to others, yet I do remember one evening when I was twelve or thirteen and we attended a Christmas party at the house of one of their friends. The children were consigned to the basement, where we were expected to amuse ourselves with games and toys, but periodically we would wander upstairs to fill our plates with food and search for sweets. When I went upstairs I stood for a moment, stricken with shyness, in the centre of the living room while the adults smiled at me and observed how I had grown. The room was strung with coloured lights, there was a tree and brightly wrapped presents, jewels on the women, loud chuckles from the men — this scene orbited around me, bleary and glamorous, and in the middle of it were my parents. They were so small! They sat on one of the sofas, looking shy and tongue-tied, plain and out of place. It was a shock to see them outside of our own home, to see how they compared to others, how they fit in the larger world.

Later in the evening, as we were getting ready to leave, I waited in the entrance of the house while my parents said their farewells upstairs. A little girl skipped past me and towards the row of shoes, boots, and high heels belonging to the hosts and their guests. She stopped in front of our family's cluster of shoes and pointed at the boots my mother had worn to the party. I can't remember what they looked like, except that they were cheap and ungainly. "Whose boots are those!" she exclaimed, laughing. "They're *so* ugly!" I think I mumbled something in agreement, and was glad that she wasn't there when my parents finally made their way downstairs and my mother pulled on her boots, oblivious. I watched her struggling with their zippers, this woman whom I had always been afraid of, whose clothes could so easily be ridiculed by a child.

Now years have passed and everyone is older. It's true: you don't believe it, but then it happens regardless, and you begin to understand the look that your middle-aged friends wear sometimes, that expression of pained surprise in their eyes, as if they woke to find themselves trapped inside faces and bodies that don't belong to the young people they really are.

Years have passed since the day I walked out of my parents' house, breaking the invisible shield around that neighbourhood. The corner store is gone, the trees along the street have grown so much that their branches almost meet over the road, forming a leafy canopy. I thought when I left home that it might be the end of my writing, the journals and poetry finally no match for the urge to leave that pounded in me until I was blind to consequence, but it was only the beginning. My writing was how I survived, for years, until gradually I began to take shape in the world independently of words, and that obsession began to loosen its hold on me. Becoming a published writer wasn't the magical thing I had envisioned, not the thing that could perfect me the way as a child I had imagined it could, but it did save me in its own way. What made it impossible to endure the family home — the writer in me that ceaselessly watched my father and mother, that responded to the tensions in the household with heartbreak — was also what made sense of everything that followed by capturing it in words.

When will it end? When I walk down the dreamlike sidewalks, the figures who silently pass all wear the masks of figures from my childhood. My friend whose father is dying is, in his customary take-charge way, choosing to deal with their traumatic relationship. He is bringing together members of his father's second and third families, facing people he has not seen since his childhood, talking about everything that happened. "Either I do this, or I end up in years and years of therapy," he said decisively. This makes sense. My admiration for him is significant. But we each make our choices and we live with their consequences. We function in the world and that, sometimes, seems like no small miracle, seems like enough — until it isn't.

I dreamt about the purple dresser again the other night. I walked into a room of my apartment and there it was, sitting squat and immovable. It dominated the room, dwarfed the other furniture, rendered my home ugly. This time, I remembered all the other dreams. And I tried to tell myself that this was a dream, too, but when I touched the dresser it was real. The lavender-painted wood under my hands, the squeaking drawers, the mess of cosmetics scattered across its scarred surface. I knew I would never be able to push it out of my apartment, not by myself — and it was clear, as it always is in these dreams, that no one could help me remove it. I looked at it this time very carefully, from every angle, running my hands along its cracked sides, removing the heavy drawers and pushing them back in, examining the ruined mirror. Still, there was nothing I could do. Once again I was left standing there, looking at the past. It had followed me into the present, and it would be there in the days and dreams that stretched ahead.

ACKNOWLEDGEMENTS

Several of these pieces first appeared, in slightly different form, in the following publications: "An Insatiable Emptiness" in *The Georgia Straight*, "Father Figures" in *Desire in Seven Voices* (Douglas & McIntyre), and "In Residence" in *Western Living*. Portions of "Anatomy of a Libel Lawsuit" first appeared in *Mix* (*The Vancouver Sun*).

With regard to "Anatomy of a Libel Lawsuit," I wish to thank the Canada Council for its assistance of a short-term grant. I am also grateful to the members of the legal profession who gave, lent, or directed me to relevant texts, engaged me in thought-provoking discussions, and encouraged me to write this piece.

237

Many thanks, finally, to my longtime agent, Denise Bukowski, and to my editor, Maya Mavjee, for her inspired suggestions.

ABOUT THE AUTHOR

Evelyn Lau has written seven books, including the bestselling short story collection *Choose Me*, published by Doubleday Canada in 1999 and Vintage Canada in 2000. *Runaway: Diary of a Street Kid*, her first book, was published in 1989 when she was eighteen. It became a Canadian bestseller (30 weeks on *The Globe and Mail* bestseller list) and has been published internationally. It was adapted into an award-winning film for television by the CBC. The short story collection, *Fresh Girls and Other Stories*, and a novel, *Other Women*, both received international acclaim. In 1992, Lau became the youngest poet ever to be nominated for the Governor General's Award, for her collection *Oedipal Dreams*. In 1999, she received a Woman of Originality Award. Evelyn Lau lives and works in Vancouver.